CURBSIDE L.A.

CURBSIDE L.A.

AN OFFBEAT GUIDE
TO THE CITY OF ANGELS
FROM THE PAGES OF
THE LOS ANGELES TIMES
BY CECILIA RASMUSSEN

Los Angeles Times

Los Angeles Times

PUBLISHER: Richard T. Schlosberg III
EDITOR: Shelby Coffey III

Los Angeles Times Syndicate

PRESIDENT AND CEO: Jesse Levine
VP/GM DOMESTIC: Steve Christensen

DIRECTOR OF BOOK DEVELOPMENT: Don Michel
EDITOR: Daniel Pollock
BOOK DESIGNER: Tom Trapnell
MAPS: Helene Webb
COVER PHOTOGRAPH: Archive Photos

Library of Congress Catalogue Number
96-007019

ISBN 1-883792-11-8
Copyright © 1996 Los Angeles Times

Published by the Los Angeles Times Syndicate
Times Mirror Square, Los Angeles, California 90053
A Times Mirror Company

FIRST PRINTING JULY 1996

Printed in the U.S.A.

....

**Editor's Note: Prices times and programs given in the book
are as of publication date, July 1996**

For Leo who asked for it.

For Patt who shaped it.

For Sheila who packaged it.

And for Bill who encouraged it.

FOREWORD

Los Angeles is often called the city where the future begins. Trends and politics, phrases and crazes, styles and delights travel from west to east and bedeck the city's reputation like flags in a massive march toward tomorrow. Cecilia Rasmussen looks at mysteries and histories of the city that provides so much of the strange stardust of the nation. She knows the sagas of the religious existentialists born in Los Angeles' desert air. She knows the haunts of the literati, and the oases for the illuminati. She knows where the crimes are committed, and where the most famous Angeleno bodies are buried. She will guide you most brilliantly through CURBSIDE L.A.

Shelby Coffey III
Editor and Executive Vice President
Los Angeles Times

CONTENTS

I.
TINSELTOWN AND GLITZBURG

S TUDIO TOURS ARE COMPULSORY FOR MANY SoCAL VISITORS. UNIVERSAL OFFERS a state-of-the-art mecca on its Studio City hilltop, with Warner Brothers and NBC just down the road in Burbank. These mega-dream factories are well worth seeing—indeed, almost impossible to avoid. But there are a dozen pioneer film studios discoverable with a little detouring from tour-bus itineraries. Check out the following pages for directions. In the process, you'll pick up some colorful backstory about the celluloid "Biz."

These days, however, studio sound stages aren't always where the real filmic action is. More and more moviemakers—for large and small screens alike—are taking to L.A. streets. We survey some favorite location spots—from the City Hall (destroyed by Martians in "War of the Worlds") to Beverly Hills' Greystone Mansion (where filming seems non-stop).

Of course, legends abound all over the mythic map of Tinseltown, wherever glamour and gossip intersect. You'll find briefings here on paparazzi (see "Shooting Stars"), the favorite hangouts of rock stars ("Down Rock 'n' Roll's Memory Lane") and writers ("Land of the Literati"), notorious Southland murders ("Scenes of the Crimes"), even celebrity graves (like Mel Blanc's, with his famous cartoon sign-off, "That's All, Folks"). And, since glamour sometimes survives the final curtain, "The Hauntings" details the after-lifestyles of the rich and famous.

Film Studios

Though most of L.A.'s pioneer film studios are gone, the buildings where the industry grew can still be visited.

1. HAMPTON STUDIOS
1041 FORMOSA AVE., HOLLYWOOD

In 1919, Charlie Chaplin, D.W. Griffith, Mary Pickford and Douglas Fairbanks Sr. formed United Artists. Three years later, Pickford and Fairbanks took over the 20-acre site. In 1938 it became Samuel Goldwyn Studios, but United Artists was still headquartered there until 1975. Ira and George Gershwin scored many of the great Goldwyn musicals that were made on the sound stage. Warner Bros. bought it in 1980. Across the street is the legendary Formosa Cafe watering hole, which served as an unofficial clubhouse for the likes of Humphrey Bogart, Marilyn Monroe and Clark Gable.

The Formosa Cafe, on the site of the old Hampton Studios in Hollywood, is a legendary watering hole once frequented by Humphrey Bogart, Marilyn Monroe and Clark Gable.

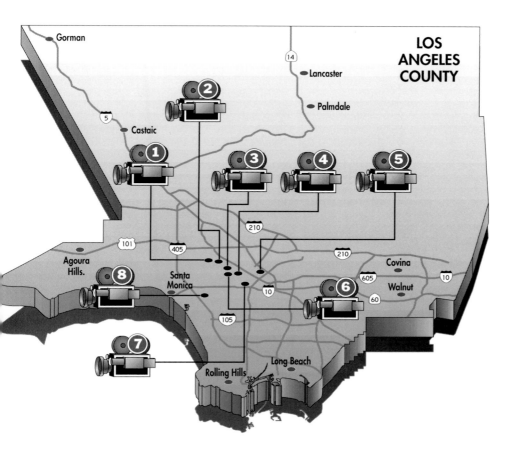

Gorman

14

Lancaster

LOS
ANGELES
COUNTY

Palmdale

5

Castaic

Agoura
Hills.

Santa
Monica

101   405

210

210

Covina

605   10

Walnut

60

105

Long Beach

Rolling Hills

2. CHARLIE CHAPLIN

1416 N. LA BREA AVE., HOLLYWOOD

Chaplin opened his own movie studio in 1918 on a peaceful street of citrus groves. The two-block compound—with its gray Colonial clapboard cottages surrounding manicured lawns and a Tudor English mansion—now houses Polygram's A&M Records. Chaplin's footprints are in the concrete in front of Stage 3.

3. DEMILLE AND LASKY BARN

2100 N. HIGHLAND AVE., HOLLYWOOD

A horse barn at Selma Avenue and Vine Street was rented in 1913 by 32-year-old Cecil B. DeMille, Samuel Goldfish (Goldwyn) and Jesse Lasky for $35 a month when they made Hollywood's first full-length motion picture, "The Squaw Man." The film cost $15,000 to make but grossed more than $200,000. The company quickly took over the entire block and later moved to Van Ness Avenue and

Mike Meadows / Los Angeles Times

The DeMille and Lasky Barn is home to the Hollywood Studio Museum.

Marathon Street, where it eventually became Paramount Studios. Paramount was housed in the barn from 1926 to 1982, when it was deeded to the preservationist group Hollywood Heritage. The barn was moved across the street from the Hollywood Bowl, restored and opened to the public, where it is dedicated to the history of the silent film era.

4. FICTION PICTURES
650 N. BRONSON AVE., HOLLYWOOD

In 1914, Adolph Zukor's Famous Players purchased a horse barn. Mary Pickford filmed "A Girl From Yesterday" there. In 1915, theater owner William H. Clune bought the studio property. Douglas Fairbanks Sr. leased the property in 1919 and built a bungalow (which is still there) and painted his name on a couple of buildings. "The Three Musketeers" and "Mark of Zorro" were filmed here in the 1920s, Walt Disney rented space in the 1930s, and the "Hopalong Cassidy" film series was shot there in 1938—as were "Superman" episodes in the 1950s.

In 1979, it became Raleigh Studio.

5. MACK SENNETT
1712 GLENDALE BLVD., ECHO PARK

The first permanent concrete-reinforced movie studio, in an area once called Edendale, gained prominence in the 1910s when Sennett, famous for his two-reel comedies, employed show-business legends Fatty Arbuckle, Gloria Swanson and Harry Langdon, the Keystone Kops and Charlie Chaplin. Here, actress Mabel Normand tossed the first custard pie in the face of actor Ben Turpin. The 35,000-square-foot building, declared a historical site in 1982, is now a storage facility owned by Public Storage Inc.

6. WARNER BROS.
5858 SUNSET BLVD., HOLLYWOOD

The Colonial mansion, built by the Warner Brothers in 1919, was later used for years as a bowling alley. The first talking picture, "The Jazz Singer" with Al Jolson, was made here in 1927. Gene Autry owned it for 18 years, after purchasing it from Paramount Pictures in 1964. Today, it's home to KTLA-TV Channel 5, and more than 50% of the original buildings remain.

7. PERALTA
5451 MARATHON ST., HOLLYWOOD

Originally located on the south side of Melrose Avenue, Peralta Studios moved across the street on Marathon in 1917, later becoming Brunton Studios, then United

Although in a new location, walk-in gate at Paramount Pictures echoes original.

Jayne Kamin-Oncea / Los Angeles Times

Studios before Paramount-Famous-Lasky took over in 1926. Paramount, the last major studio remaining in Hollywood, was home to such greats as Mary Pickford, Claudette Colbert, Mae West, Clara Bow, Bob Hope, Bing Crosby and Dorothy Lamour. A stage built in 1919 still remains, along with Paramount's original walk-in gate and administration building.

8. TRIANGLE PICTURES
10202 WASHINGTON BLVD., CULVER CITY

With land and financing supplied in part by Harry Culver, Tom Ince built this studio in 1915. Later it was purchased by Goldwyn and in 1924 it became MGM. Many of the original structures are still there, including the historic gate marked by the classical columns, the Yellow Brick Road that made its way to Oz, the rehearsal studio of Fred Astaire and Gene Kelly, and the side entrance of the administration building, where Spencer Tracy supposedly first met Katharine Hepburn. In 1991, the studio was renamed Sony Pictures Entertainment.

Sony Pictures Entertainment on Washington Boulevard in Culver City was once Triangle Pictures.

Tony Barnard / Los Angeles Times

Film Locations

From City Hall to Batman's Mansion—L.A. County
locales that keep showing up in movies and on TV.

1. THE BEVERLY HILLBILLIES' HOUSE
ST. CLOUD & BEL AIR ROADS, BEL AIR

From 1962 to 1970, this home on Bel Air Road near Beverly Hills served as the stomping grounds for the Clampett clan, an Ozark Mountains family that struck it rich with an oil well in their front yard and moved to Beverly Hills, looking for "swimming pools, movie stars." The mansion is next door to former President Ronald Reagan's. Other neighbors include Zsa Zsa Gabor and Elizabeth Taylor.

2. GREYSTONE PARK
905 LOMA VISTA DR., BEVERLY HILLS

The Doheny Mansion at 905 Loma Vista Dr., also known as Greystone Park, is by far the most popular mansion ever filmed in Beverly Hills. This magnificent 55-room, gray limestone building, with walls three feet thick, was built by oil magnate

Interior of Doheny mansion, "Greystone Park," in Beverly Hills, featured in "Ghostbusters II" and "The Witches of Eastwick."

Edward L. Doheny in 1928 for his only son, Edward Lawrence (Ned) Doheny Jr. The estate once occupied 415 acres. Just a few months after the younger Doheny moved into the humble 46,054-square-foot abode with his wife and five children, both he and his male secretary were found dead in Doheny's bedroom. Some say the secretary shot Doheny because he was denied a raise, then turned the gun on himself. But published reports at the time suggested that Doheny and his secretary were lovers and that Doheny fired both shots because he was afraid his family would find out about his affair.

In 1965 the city of Beverly Hills bought Greystone mansion

Larry Davis / Los Angeles Times

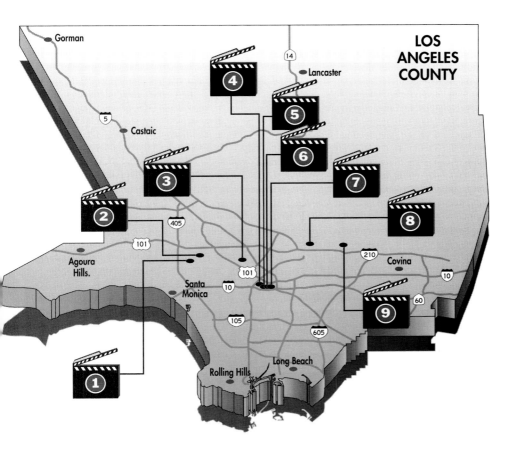

and 18.3 surrounding acres. The rest of the land was purchased by Paul Trousdale, developer of Trousdale Estates. The mansion served as a backdrop in such films as "The Golden Child," "Ghostbusters II," "Jumping Jack Flash," "The Witches of East-wick," "Native Son" and "The Marrying Man." Television viewers may have seen it in "The Winds of War," "Murder, She Wrote," "MacGyver," "General Hospital" or "Dark Shadows."

Approximately 30 films are shot at Greystone annually, according to a mansion spokesman. To film the exterior and interior at Greystone costs roughly $9,090 per day. The Beverly Hills Department of Parks and Recreation reaps the benefits.

3. GRIFFITH PARK OBSERVATORY
2800 E. OBSERVATORY ROAD, LOS ANGELES

The teen-age outlaw of a previous generation, legendary actor James Dean, gave it his all in "Rebel Without a Cause" in 1955. In the film, Dean loitered at the Griffith Park Observatory, and today a bust of Dean stands on the west front lawn. The observatory was also the home of several key scenes from "The Terminator," "Dragnet," "Battlestar Galactica," "Earth Girls Are Easy" and "The Rocketeer." Scenes for television's "The Colbys," "Bionic Woman" and "Wonder Woman" were also filmed there.

4. HERALD EXAMINER BUILDING
1111 S. BROADWAY, LOS ANGELES

Since the Hearst Corp. pulled the plug on the Herald Examiner newspaper in November, 1989, the Julia Morgan-designed building has portrayed fictional headquarters in TV and movies, including police stations in the 1990 cop-thrillers "The Rookie" starring Clint Eastwood and Charlie Sheen and "Rainbow Drive" starring Peter Weller. Other filmings at the abandoned newspaper building have included the 1995 movie "The Usual Suspects" starring Kevin Spacey, who won the supporting actor award for his role as a deceptive criminal; the 1995 hyperkinetic thriller about L.A. "Strange Days" starring Angela Bassett and "Cable Guy" starring Jim Carrey. TV crews have been busy there on such programs as Fox's "Alien Nation," NBC's "Mancuso, F.B.I.," the ABC pilot of "K-9" and NBC's "Shannon's Deal." Commercials for IBM computers, AT&T long distance, Cover Girl cosmetics and Jockey Underwear have also used the premises.
   ■ "Hearst's Newspaper Castle," see Page 11.

5. BRADBURY BUILDING
304 S. BROADWAY, LOS ANGELES

This spectacular 1893 office building, the new home of the Los Angeles Police Department's Internal Affairs Division, is no stranger to law enforcement. L.A. cop Harrison Ford searched for some 21st-century androids in the downtown landmark in the 1982 "Blade Runner." And 1930s gumshoe Wayne Rogers kept an office there in the 1976 TV series "City of Angels."

Five stories' worth of lace-like, wrought-iron balcony railings, open elevator cages and twisted staircases, bathed in light filtered through a skylight, also provided key interiors for such films as "Wolf," featuring Jack Nicholson and Michelle Pfeiffer (1994); "Greedy," with Michael J. Fox and Kirk Douglas (1994), and the Christian Slater-Kevin Bacon movie "Murder in the First" (1995).

This century-old building has also been in the spotlight for fictional and real-life roles, housing the famous Ross Cutlery shop, another macabre landmark, that sold a 15-inch Stiletto knife to one-time murder suspect O.J. Simpson.

6. CITY HALL
200 N. SPRING ST., LOS ANGELES

City Hall has starred in more movies and television series than most Hollywood actors. From October, 1989, to October, 1990, City Hall, inside and out, appeared in almost 100 productions. And City Hall has proved itself to be a star with real lasting power. Just after its completion in 1928, the year "talkies" were introduced, actor Lon Chaney starred in MGM's whodunit "While the City Sleeps," which featured several City Hall shots.

Through the years, City Hall continued to play supporting roles, appearing in

The Bradbury Building: five stories' worth of wrought-iron balcony railings, open elevator cages and twisted staircases.

R.L. Oliver / Los Angeles Times

such films as "Mildred Pierce" (1945), "War of the Worlds" (1953), "D.O.A." (1949) and more recently in "Protocol," "Seems Like Old Times," "48 Hours," "Another 48 Hours" and "Death Warrant."

On the smaller screen, it served as the Daily Planet building in the "Superman" television series. Although it was destroyed by Martians in "War of the Worlds," it somehow survived to portray the U.S. Capitol in "The Jimmy Hoffa Story" and the Vatican in "The Thorn Birds." You might also have caught a glimpse of City Hall in the series "Kojak," "Cagney and Lacey," "The Rockford Files," "Matlock," "Hill Street Blues," "L.A. Law," "Equal Justice," "The Trials of Rosie O'Neill" and "The Big One: The Great Los Angeles Earthquake."

7. UNION STATION
800 N. ALAMEDA ST., LOS ANGELES

With its black walnut beams, ancient Venetian blinds, multicolored tiles adorned with parrots, 3,000-pound chandeliers and marble mosaic walkway, Union Station remains remarkably intact after a little more than half a century. The film that used the station most extensively was the aptly named 1950 movie "Union Station," which starred William Holden. Other well-known films shot there were "The Way We Were" (1972), "Gable and Lombard" (1975), "Oh God! Book II" (1980) and "Blade Runner" (1982) and the TV series "Hunter" (1990).

■ "Chinatown and Union Station," see Page 12.

8. WAYNE MANOR, BATMAN'S HAUNT
300 BLOCK SOUTH SAN RAFAEL AVENUE, PASADENA

Hidden behind a 6-foot-high wall is the three-story Tudor mansion—complete with massive mahogany stairway and butler's pantry—that was known as Wayne

Tudor mansion in Pasadena served as Wayne Manor in the 1960s TV series "Batman."

Lou Mack / Los Angeles Times

Manor in the "Batman" television series. In 1966, at the beginning of the show's two-year run, external shots of the house were filmed, but most of the action occurred on a sound stage. The cost was $1,500 a day for the three days of filming. The most recent filming there was for "Dead Again."

9. QUEEN ANNE COTTAGE
301 N. BALDWIN AVE., ARCADIA

The cottage was built over a century ago by the flamboyant millionaire E. J. (Lucky) Baldwin, then 56, as a wedding present for his fourth bride, 16-year-old Lillie Bennett. But the house was not completed until after the pair had married and separated.

It starred in "Fantasy Island," from 1978 until 1984, when the studio built its own replica.

"Fantasy Island" featured Queen Anne Cottage at Los Angeles State and County Arboretum, where several Tarzan movies were filmed.

Cassy Cohen / Los Angeles Times

The Los Angeles State and County Arboretum in Arcadia, where the cottage is located, has provided a setting for more than 200 films. Johnny Weissmuller swung through the arboretum trees in five Tarzan films. Such oldies as the "Road to Singapore" and "Safari" were also filmed there. Television shows that have filmed scenes there include "L.A. Law," "Murder, She Wrote," "Unsolved Mysteries," "Dallas," "Falcon

Crest" and "MacGyver." On a sliding scale, studios are charged $1,500 to $3,900 per day and commercials run $1,500 to $2,500 per day.

___

SOURCES: "Movie Lover's Guide to Hollywood," by Richard Alleman, Cast Locations, City Hall, Leslie Halliwell's Film Guide and film coordinators from various cities.

Hearst's Newspaper Castle

It was one of the first architectural jewels in the publishing crown of America's most flamboyant press lord, William Randolph Hearst. And although it sits abandoned today, it once was home to one of Hearst's journalistic triumphs.

For 86 years, the modified Mission Revival-style headquarters at 11th Street and Broadway housed the Los Angeles Examiner (and later the Herald Examiner), one of half a dozen or more newspapers that heralded the daily comings and goings of a burgeoning Los Angeles. It served up a brew of news, political insight, scandal and gossip.

The building brought such delight to its owner that Hearst decided to entrust the construction of his legendary castle in San Simeon to its architect, a woman in a profession then dominated by men.

Julia Morgan was ideally suited to the task. A perfectionist with a passion for quality detail, she designed more than 700 buildings in a career that covered over half a century.

In the Examiner, Morgan offered Hearst a hand-painted, tiled lobby of gold and marble and a private apartment upstairs for his personal use. The block-long

Ornate lobby of the Herald Examiner.

Los Angeles Times

The Herald-Examiner building, now vacant, sits in the shadow of high rises.

Iris Schneider / Los Angeles Times

structure on a half-acre was set off with colorful domes at each corner.

This building, which was added to the city's list of historic cultural monuments in 1977, has been vacant since then. Today, it is used occasionally by movie crews.

Chinatown and Union Station

Los Angeles' Chinese community began to develop in 1859, when laborers were brought in to build a wagon road near Newhall and later the railroads. By 1890, the population had grown to about 2,000, concentrated in about 43 acres bounded by Alameda, Macy, Lyon and Aliso streets.

By the turn of the century, Chinatown's narrow, unpaved, dimly lit streets and alleys had become a residential and commercial community. Within its confines were about 200 buildings, including a Chinese opera house, a school, restaurants, three temples, a newspaper, a telephone company and a produce market.

Chinatown also attracted the city's non-Chinese, who would go to eat in the restaurants. Some of the city's businessmen availed themselves of Chinatown's less savory attractions—gambling, whorehouses and opium dens.

Immigrants paid rent to the family of rancher Juan Apablasa, who owned most of Old Chinatown. By 1913, the family was taking in a then-hefty $4,000 a month from Chinese tenants, according to a June, 1949, account in the Los Angeles Times.

The threat of relocation began in 1915, when the city proposed a new terminal on Apablasa's property for three separate railroads: the Southern Pacific, Union Pacific and Atchison, Topeka & Santa Fe—hence the name Union Station.

It took almost three decades of legal battles among the city, the railroads and the Apablasas, but finally officials evicted about 3,000 Chinese residents.

Twenty-eight Chinese men and women soon pooled their money, gathered their belongings and created another enclave nearby, on vacant railroad property between Bernard, North Hill and College streets and Broadway.

To get around laws barring land ownership by non-natives, the group, later known as "the founders," formed a corporation through their native-born children and bought railroad property, with the covert help of Herbert Lapham, a sympathetic railway agent. On June 25, 1938, they opened New Chinatown, with 18 stores and a bean cake factory.

But the city had its own alternative for the displaced Chinese. The same month New Chinatown opened, a tourist attraction called China City opened at Ord and Spring streets. China City, like Olvera Street, was the brainchild of activist Christine Sterling.

Los Angeles Times

This 1937 photo shows the tower of Union Station rising above Old Chinatown in Ferguson Alley.

A set designer from Paramount collaborated in its conception, and movie mogul Cecil B. DeMille donated props and costumes from the 1937 movie "The Good Earth." Although the Chinese community was grateful, members of the corporation in New Chinatown thought the theatrical display with serpentine streets and rickshaws was foolish and impractical.

They were right. The "Celestial Empire" of China City was destroyed by fire 11 years later and never rebuilt.

Alameda Street looking northeast in 1947, with Union Station in the background.

Los Angeles Times

Shooting Stars

Paparazzi stalk and shoot celebs at bars, clubs, eateries; a short list of their favorite, glitzy, hunting hangouts.

Federico Fellini popularized the term "paparazzi" in his 1959 movie "La Dolce Vita." The film's most insolent photographer is named Signor Paparazzo. In Italian, paparazzi roughly means "household pests."

Our local flock of brazen shutterbugs, who provide a steady flow of celebrity snapshots to the tabloids, know where to find Hollywood's stars day and night.

These days, besides taking still shots of the stars, many paparazzi juggle video cameras in hopes of selling footage to television programs. Helicopters and parachutes have also become tools of the trade for a few daring photographers who seek shots of high-security celebrity weddings.

More hazardous duty: Paparazzi have been at the receiving end of more than a few celebrity fists, including those of Sean Penn and Alec Baldwin.

Is it worth it? Well, some glitzy pictures have fetched five or even six figures. Reportedly, a shot of Sylvester Stallone with fist raised sold for about $50,000, and one pregnant-bikini photo of Princess Diana brought $100,000.

In hopes of this kind of bonanza, photographers spend long hours on celebrity stakeouts. They befriend stars and develop connections with parking valets, maitre d's, club bouncers and airline reservation clerks. While they won't disclose all their favorite local hangouts, they did volunteer the following:

Zsa Zsa Gabor at the Beverly Hills Courthouse in 1989.

Robert Durrell / Los Angeles Times

Eateries

DAN TANA'S, WEST HOLLYWOOD

Older crowd, but was also a favorite hangout for the late Sam Kinison. It is said to be Magic Johnson's favorite restaurant. Dabney Coleman and Bruce Springsteen are also reported to be customers here.

FORUM CLUB, INGLEWOOD

When there's a game or a concert or fight night at the Great Western Forum, it's a good place to catch the Lakers and other celebrities, from Jack Nicholson to Michael J. Fox to Magic Johnson.

HOLLYWOOD ATHLETIC CLUB, HOLLYWOOD

Steve Dorff of "Major Dad," Luke Perry, Jason Priestley and Grant Show of "Melrose Place," along with other '90s brat packers, come to eat, drink and shoot pool.

THE IVY, WEST HOLLYWOOD

Attracts Madonna, Goldie Hawn, Elizabeth Taylor, Cher, Olivia Newton John, Bruce Springsteen.

Arnold Schwarzenegger at the opening of the Ronald Reagan Library in Simi Valley in 1991.

Alan Hagman / Los Angeles Times

JERRY'S FAMOUS DELI, STUDIO CITY

A late-night hangout for the likes of Arsenio Hall, Eddie Murphy and Charlie Sheen. Popular with kids from both the '80s and '90s brat packs.

KATE MANTILINI, BEVERLY HILLS

Late at night, a place where celebs can be seen munching burgers.

LE DOME, WEST HOLLYWOOD

Warren Beatty, Jack Nicholson, Mickey Rourke, Michael Jackson and Elizabeth Taylor are said to frequent the restaurant. Celebrities use the back door to avoid being photographed.

PATINA, LOS ANGELES

Celebs such as Mary Hart, Ed Harris, Warren Beatty, Diane Keaton and Kareem Abdul-Jabbar may be seen munching caviar-topped blini.

POLO LOUNGE, BEVERLY HILLS

Used to be a great place to photograph such celebrities as Ronald Reagan and Charles Bronson at Sunday brunch, but now security is too tight for most paparazzi.

SCHATZIE'S, SANTA MONICA

Arnold Schwarzenegger and Maria Shriver's deli attracts many Westside celebs.

72 MARKET STREET, VENICE

Dudley Moore is part owner.

SPAGO, WEST HOLLYWOOD

Local paparazzi claim Wolfgang Puck's place is now just another tourist attraction—"the next stop after Mann's Chinese Theater." Photographers say it was the place to be seen in the 1980s, the era of nighttime soap operas. In those days, as many as 30 paparazzi would line the sidewalk and driveway in front of the restaurant in hopes of getting a picture of Joan Collins or someone from the cast of "Dallas."

Clubs

Many top L.A. clubs that celebrities frequent have a short life span. They're hot for six months and then disappear. A couple of the known spots at the moment:

Balistics/Whiskey-A-Go-Go: One night per week the Whiskey goes "Balistics," thanks to David Faustino (Budd on Fox's "Married With Children"), who takes over the Whiskey to operate a dance club for the under-21 crowd. On some Thursday nights, young celebs, including Barbra Streisand's son, Jason Gould, and Kirk Cameron's sister, Candace, show up.

Bar-One, West Hollywood: Attracts patrons such as Don Johnson, Ringo Starr, George Harrison and Warren Beatty. Since it is a restaurant as well as a bar, some under-age celebrities also show up there.

Shopping

RODEO DRIVE

Most celebs enter stores through back entrances, and arrange to shop at off hours and have purchases delivered. However, the likes of Elizabeth Taylor and Charles Bronson have been seen strolling along the street.

SHERMAN OAKS GALLERIA

Valley celebs drop in to shop.

Hospitals

CEDARS-SINAI

Its reputation as a quality medical facility, along with its proximity to Beverly Hills, assures its status as a celebrity center.

ST. JOHN'S

There is a VIP section where Hollywood celebs such as Michael Jackson and Elizabeth Taylor get treatment.

All Around Town

ANYWHERE IN BEVERLY HILLS

Including places such as the post office, where the last picture of Fred Astaire was taken.

ACADEMY OF MOTION PICTURE ARTS & SCIENCES

Screenings at the Academy are a good bet to bring out the stars. However, often celebs RSVP and give the tickets to friends and family.

BIKER HANGOUTS

Members of the biker crowd, including Mickey Rourke, Billy Idol, Keanu Reeves, Amanda Bearse (Marcy on "Married With Children"), Prince, Eddie Murphy, Dennis Hopper, Peter Fonda and members of the bands Poison and Motley Crue can sometimes be seen at the Rock Store on Mulholland Drive and at the Roxbury.

DIRECTORS GUILD OF AMERICA

Like the Academy, a good place to shoot the stars. It's possible to catch Barbra Streisand and others here.

HOLLYWOOD BILLIARDS

Kiefer Sutherland is said to have spent several nights here playing out his sorrow after his breakup with Julia Roberts. Other pool-hall celebs include Keanu Reeves and Anthony Kiedis of the Red Hot Chili Peppers.

CRISTOPHE HAIR SALON BEVERLY HILLS

Hillary Clinton, Sally Field, Ellen Barkin, Steven Spielberg and Bruce Springsteen get their dos done here.

LAX

Because of tight security at the airport, one of the few places that paparazzi can get shots of the celebs without makeup, looking disheveled and frumpy, is at the luggage pickup area.

Hollywood Athletic Club

Since it was built in 1923, the Hollywood Athletic Club on Sunset Boulevard has housed a men's gym—which accounts for its name—a Jewish university, a Russian nightclub and, now, a pool hall.

About a century ago, gambling halls, billiard dens and saloons were prohibited in the God-fearing community of Hollywood. In 1905, the Los Angeles Times described the area as a place where "the saloon and its kindred evils are unknown."

Little did the righteous residents know that the movie industry would

Marc Wanamaker Bison Archives

The Hollywood Athletic Club during its glory days in the late 1920s.

soon move in, and Hollywood's conservative churchgoers would find themselves dwelling amid a "troupe of scalawags," recalled humorist Anita Loos, screenwriter and author of "Gentlemen Prefer Blondes."

But the "scalawags" joined forces with the good citizens of Hollywood—at least the male half—and launched a membership drive to build the Hollywood Athletic Club. A million dollars later, the nine-story club, then Hollywood's tallest building, opened on New Year's Eve, 1923.

The gym's fencing instructor was Cornel Wilde, before he was "discovered" by some of the stars he was hired to teach. Buster Crabbe, the club's lifeguard, trained in the swimming pool to win a 1932 Olympic gold medal. He later starred as the futuristic sex symbol, Flash Gordon. Crabbe would also share "Tarzan" movie role duties with another club habitue and Olympic gold medalist, actor Johnny Weismuller.

For more than 30 years, the Hollywood Athletic Club remained the private watering hole, crash pad, game room, gymnasium, lunchroom and retreat for its members, among them such notables as John Barrymore, Errol Flynn, William Powell, W.C. Fields, John Wayne, Charlie Chaplin, Clark Gable and Anthony Quinn. Rudolph Valentino kept a permanent bachelor pad there.

During Prohibition, liquor was dispensed in teacups at the club's formal dances. All-night drinking parties flourished in the penthouse.

At one party, Wayne stood on the penthouse balcony and hurled billiard balls at cars; Barrymore reputedly climbed atop the roof, where the Fire Department had to rescue him.

One local old-timer remembered the night Wayne and a producer took bets on who was better at punching his fist through doors. The next day, the club presented the winner—Wayne—with a bill for $2,000.

Al Jolson recorded "I'm California Dreaming" in the gymnasium. In 1931, Tyrone Power Sr., the great Shakespearean stage actor and silent-screen star, died in his upstairs room in the arms of his 17-year-old son, Tyrone Jr.

The same year, Walt Disney's plunge into debt drove him to the edge of a breakdown. But after several weeks of recuperating at the club, with vigorous workouts in the gym, Disney bounced back and soon commanded an entertainment empire.

After World War II, the club began to deteriorate. In 1958, it was reborn as the West Coast branch of the Jewish Theological Seminary. It later became the University of Judaism, where high school and college students took evening classes.

In 1979, the institution moved away, and the tower was leased out for offices; the bottom floor briefly housed a Russian nightclub and restaurant.

Then, in 1989, entrepreneur Tom Salter leased the 70-year-old building and put $1.3 million into reviving its glamour. Its refurbished plush wood and velvet interior and restored Spanish/Mediterranean-style exterior have enticed new stars: tabloid regulars such as Madonna and Kiefer Sutherland, as well as Charlie Sheen, Kathleen Turner, Eric Clapton, Axl Rose and Kevin Costner, often dine and pick up a pool cue on the premises.

But so far no one has punched in a single door.

The Schwab's Legend

When Jack Schwab bought a failing drugstore at 8024 Sunset Blvd. in 1932, he took note of the movie studios in the vicinity—RKO, Republic and Columbia—and saw the future. Schwab's drugstore went on to become Hollywood's prime hangout for underemployed actors, directors, screenwriters and aspiring stars.

Charge accounts and check cashing were its early innovations. Later, a paging system and a special phone for incoming calls was installed for the famous and the near-famous. Waitresses were hired to fit the role of the sympathetic matron, and were noted as much for their abilities as amateur psychologists as for counter skills.

Despite popular belief, Lana Turner was not discovered here spooning an ice-cream soda. She was sipping a Coke in a malt shop on Sunset across from Hollywood High School. But Schwab's had plenty of genuine glamour.

Among its patrons were Judy Garland, the Marx brothers, Sylvester Stallone, Martha Raye, Robert Taylor, Danny Thomas, Goldie Hawn, Al Pacino, Shelley Winters, Cesar Romero, Ed McMahon, Clark Gable and a host of others. Charlie Chaplin got behind the soda fountain to make his own milk shakes. Ava Gardner put on an apron and served customers ice-cream sodas. Hugh O'Brian worked as a soda jerk. F. Scott Fitzgerald had a heart attack while buying cigarettes here. And Gloria Swanson came to Schwab's to buy her makeup.

Then there were the legends. In 1939, composer Harold Arlen was walking by Schwab's when, it is said, he was inspired by the light coming from the drugstore windows to write "Over the Rainbow."

Writing from an office on the premises, Hollywood columnist Sidney Skolsky had a monthly feature in a movie magazine called "From a Stool at Schwab's." Skolsky once said that "at Schwab's they operate on the notion that Joe Doakes is just as important to Joe Doakes as Lana Turner is to Lana Turner."

The soda fountain where Hollywood legends were born and new stars discovered closed its doors for the last time on Oct. 23, 1983.

The auctioneer's gavel sounded on Dec. 7 of that year, when everything that was not bolted down went to the highest bidder. The large red and blue sign over the front door sold for $650 and the smaller one on the roof went for $200; for $500 a Beverly Hills investment banker got the pharmacy's Rolodex files, containing the names and addresses of every person who had an account with Schwab's, and the leather and canvas payroll bag sold for $300.

Almost a decade later, a 160,000-square-foot Italian Renaissance-style entertainment mall was raised on the site.

Schwab's drugstore on Sunset Boulevard shortly before it closed on Oct. 23, 1983.

Rick Meyer / Los Angeles Times

Land of Literati

L.A. has been celebrated and vilified in fiction. Here are a dozen spots inhabited by writers or their characters.

----

1. ALEX ABELLA
DOWNTOWN JEWELRY DISTRICT

A Spanish-language interpreter in Los Angeles Superior Court and the author of "Killing of the Saints" (1991), Abella portrays through the eyes of his protagonist, Charles Morrell, the city's legal, criminal, ethnic and racial subcultures. The opening scene describes robbers driving a De Soto to the scene of their crime at "Schnitzer Jewelers," at 6th and Hill streets: "The car made quite a sight, its sky blue aerodynamic hood and fenders and shiny chrome torpedo bumpers muscling through downtown rush hour traffic, as conspicuous as a Whittier Boulevard cholo strutting down Hill in flying colors with his ruca on his arm."

2. CHRISTOPHER ISHERWOOD
145 ADELAIDE, SANTA MONICA

The novelist and outspoken gay-rights advocate had a tartly damning vision of Los Angeles in "A Single Man" (1964). "He stops the car and stands at the road's rough yellow dirt edge, beside a manzanita bush, and looks out over Los Angeles like a sad Jewish prophet of doom, as he takes a leak. Babylon is fallen, that great city. But this city is not great, was never great, and has nearly no distance to fall."

3. RAYMOND CHANDLER
12216 SHETLAND LANE, BRENTWOOD

Chandler's style revealed an intense love-hate relationship with Los Angeles, where he lived from 1912 to 1946. At times, he evoked a wistful, affectionate attitude in his private detective hero, Philip Marlowe, a kind of an urban knight who struggled to be honest in a corrupt city. While Chandler lived at the Brentwood address, his character lived on the cliffs above High Tower Drive in Hollywood Heights, in a building with a fancy elevator tower described in "The High Window" and the movie version of "The Long Goodbye." In "The Big Sleep," the Santa Monica Municipal Pier is called the Bay City Pier, and it is from here that Marlowe and others catch a launch to an offshore gambling ship. There is no mistaking Malibu in the description of Montemar Vista in "Farewell, My Lovely," nor "the violet light at the top of Bullock's green-tinged tower"—the old Bullocks Wilshire.

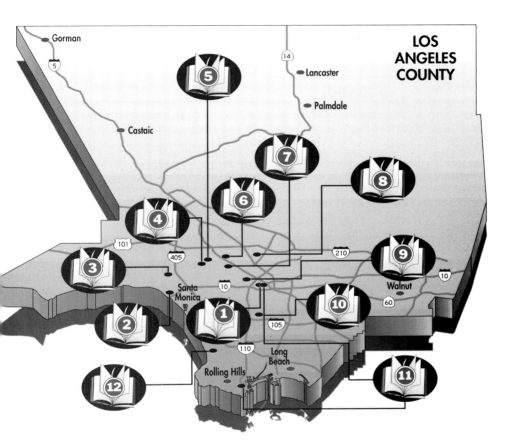

LOS ANGELES COUNTY

Gorman
Lancaster
Palmdale
Castaic
Santa Monica
Walnut
Long Beach
Rolling Hills

Steve Dykes / Los Angeles Times

Raymond Chandler's private detective hero Philip Marlowe lived in the cliffs above High Tower Drive in the Hollywood Heights.

21

4. ALDOUS HUXLEY
740 N. KINGS ROAD, LOS ANGELES

Best known for "Brave New World," Huxley lived in California when he wrote "Ape and Essence" (1948). It is the ultimate horror vision—but one not without humor—of Los Angeles in the year 2018. Mutant survivors of an atomic war gather in Pershing Square, across the street from their temple at the Biltmore Hotel. Heat for communal ovens is provided by the burning of books taken from the nearby public library. The main event of the year is held at the Biltmore—a wild two-week orgy; sex is outlawed the rest of the year.

5. JOAN DIDION
SUNSET AND LA BREA

The author places the still center of the turning world at the corner of Sunset and La Brea in "Play It As It Lays" (1970), a decade or so before everything around that intersection was leveled for mini-malls. Didion's heroine, Maria Wyeth, roams the freeways in a Corvette, or the Ferrari she took from an actor who beat her up. "Again and again she returned to an intricate stretch just south of the interchange where successful passage from the Hollywood onto the Harbor required a diagonal move across four lanes of traffic. On the afternoon she finally did it without once braking or once losing the beat on the radio she was exhilarated...."

6. JAMES M. CAIN
6301 QUEBEC ST., HOLLYWOOD HILLS

The classic novel "Double Indemnity" (1936) uses the distinctive features of Spanish Colonial Revival architecture to set the scene for this drama of lust and murder. "It didn't look like a House of Death when I saw it. It was just a Spanish house, like all the rest of them in California, with white walls, red tile roof, and a patio out to one side. It was built cockeyed. The garage was under the house, the first floor was over that, and the rest of it was spilled up the hill any way they could get it in."

7. NATHANAEL WEST
1817 IVAR AVE., HOLLYWOOD

"The Day of the Locust" (1939) was inspired by a hot, terrible summer of 1935 that West spent in this Hollywood boardinghouse, at the height of the Depression, when he was broke and suffering from gonorrhea and prostate problems. The fires in the Hollywood Hills that summer forever colored his perception of Los Angeles. West wrote that in the rooming house, which he named "Chateau Mirabella," the halls "reeked of antiseptic," and that "another name for Ivar Street was Lysol Alley." Whitley Avenue was the street where patent medicine was sold, and Grauman's Chinese Theater (now Mann's) was the setting for the violent conclusion.

8. EVELYN WAUGH
FOREST LAWN IN GLENDALE

This English gentleman was the author of the satirical novel "The Loved One" (1948). The book followed a 1947 visit to Hollywood, and Waugh, appalled by Southern California in general and Forest Lawn Cemetery in particular, set most of the book in "Whispering Glades," a thinly disguised Forest Lawn.

Nathanael West, 1817 Ivar Ave., Hollywood.

Lacy Atkins / Los Angeles Times

9. JUDITH FREEMAN
MACARTHUR PARK

In "The Chinchilla Farm" (1990), the writer explores the crime and drug-plagued neighborhood. "One day, returning from work, I was walking through the park when I saw a man lying face down near a fountain. His belongings were stuffed

23

MacArthur Park.

into plastic bags surrounding him on the grass. From somewhere came the sound of a baby bird, the unmistakably frantic chirpings of distress, like the protests of a small chick separated from its mother.... How could he sleep, I wondered, with the constant sounds of distress filling his ears?"

10. ARNA BONTEMPS
WATTS

One of the nation's most important black writers of his time tells what it was like growing up in Watts in his novel "Anyplace But Here." Bontemps traces the evolution of black ghettos, making Watts his "Mudtown." He recalls fond childhood memories as well as problems of going to school and working nights at the post office in the early 1900s. He writes with special pleasure of New Orleans jazz greats such as Jelly Roll Morton, whose Los Angeles heyday was in the 1930s. He waxes nostalgic over pre-World War II Watts, when "Los Angeles in legend became 'paradise west' to Negroes still languishing in Egyptland of the south."

11. JACK KEROUAC
FLOPHOUSES, DOWNTOWN AND SAN PEDRO

Kerouac was the King of the Beats—the eternal wanderer. "Lonesome Traveler" (1961) begins with Kerouac arriving in Los Angeles on a train called the "Zipper," a play on the train named Zephyr. From a hotel on Main Street, he looks out at the "hot sunny streets of Los Angeles Christmas." That same night, another hotel, this one in San Pedro, "had potted palms and potted barfronts and cars parked, and everything dead and windless with the dead California sad windless smokesmog."

12. ROBINSON JEFFERS
HERMOSA BEACH

The last of the great narrative poets was mostly associated with Big Sur. Although Jeffers lived most of his younger years in Highland Park, Pasadena and Long Beach, he also frequented several bars along Spring Street during the early 1900s. Imbued with a passion for nature, Jeffers wrote about the San Gabriel Mountains. He also lived in Hermosa Beach and wrote movingly in "At Playa Hermosa" of a place having neither "despair nor hope."

SOURCE: "Literary L.A." and "In Search of Literary L.A." by Lionel Rolfe.

Scenes of the Crimes

Some of L.A.'s notorious crimes—solved and unsolved—
have spawned books, movies, even sightseeing tours.

1. DOROTHY STRATTEN
10881 CLARKSON ROAD, WEST LOS ANGELES

Playboy magazine's 1980 "Playmate of the Year," 20-year-old Dorothy Stratten, was raped and murdered by her estranged husband Paul Snider in his rented two-story stucco house in the shadow of the Santa Monica freeway. The killing, on Aug. 14, 1980, reportedly occurred after Snider had learned that his wife was having an affair with director Peter Bogdanovich. Snider then turned the 12-gauge shotgun on himself.

Dorothy Stratten, 1980 "Playmate of the Year," murdered by estranged husband, Paul Snider.

2. NICOLE BROWN SIMPSON AND RONALD LYLE GOLDMAN
875 S. BUNDY DR., BRENTWOOD

On the night of June 12, 1994, after a celebratory supper at a nearby restaurant, the bodies of Nicole Brown Simpson, 35, the mother of two and ex-wife of football great O.J. Simpson, and Ronald Lyle Goldman, a 25-year-old waiter at the same restaurant, Mezzaluna, were found stabbed to death.

Goldman had been cornered by his attacker, trapped in a cage of trees and railings. The killer had drawn a blade across his neck, twice—then slashed his throat and lungs. Nicole, who may have been knocked out first with a blunt blow to the head, died from a long, deep slice to her neck that severed arteries and nicked her spinal cord. Then, as she slumped on the ground, the killer may have pulled back her hair to bare her throat, which was cut nearly from ear to ear.

O.J. Simpson, accused of the murders, was found not guilty on Oct. 3, 1995, ending his 15 months in jail.

3. 'VAMPING VENUS'
17575 PACIFIC COAST HIGHWAY, MALIBU

Actress and comedian Thelma Todd, known as the "Vamping Venus," was found dead Dec. 15, 1935, slumped over the steering wheel of her convertible in a

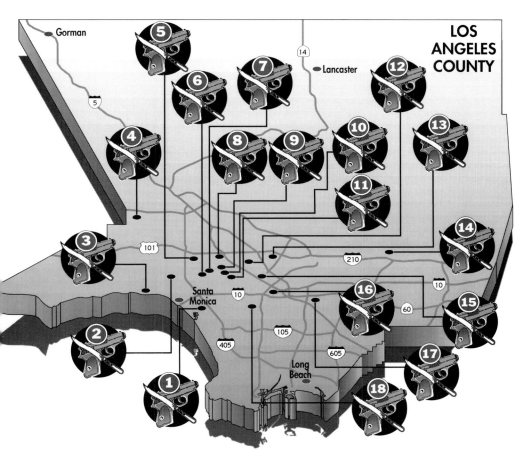

LOS
ANGELES
COUNTY

Gorman

Lancaster

Santa
Monica

Long
Beach

garage above her Malibu restaurant. Her death was ruled a suicide, but some believe it was murder. Toddy's Cafe is now a publishing company.

4. SHORTY SHEA
SPAHN MOVIE RANCH, 12000 SANTA SUSANA PASS ROAD, CHATSWORTH

Donald (Shorty) Shea disappeared one day in 1969 from this rugged acreage where Charles Manson and his homicidal band lived for a time amid broken-down sets once used in Western movies. Police believe that Shea, who worked on the ranch as a wrangler, was decapitated and buried somewhere

Thelma Todd, actress and comedian known as the "Vamping Venus," found dead above her Malibu restaurant in 1935.

on the property. His remains have never been found. The ranch has since been subdivided into several parcels.

5. SHARON TATE
10050 CIELO DR., BENEDICT CANYON

The quiet of Benedict Canyon was broken over several hours by screams and gunshots on the night of Aug. 9, 1969. Actress Sharon Tate, who was 8 1/2 months pregnant, and four other victims were beaten, stabbed and shot. The word "PIGS" was scrawled on the front door in Tate's blood. Charlie Manson and his bizarre cult members were found guilty of this gruesome slaughter.

The house has since been torn down, but a store on Sunset Boulevard, "You've Got Bad Taste," sells pieces of dry wall from the wreckage, along with a map and house diagram, for $2.50. All profits are donated to AIDS charities.

6. JOHNNY STOMPANATO
730 N. BEDFORD DR., BEVERLY HILLS

On Good Friday in 1958, actress Lana Turner's abusive boyfriend, organized crime figure Johnny Stompanato, was stabbed to death in Turner's pink bedroom by her 14-year-old daughter, Cheryl Crane. The killing was ruled justifiable homicide and no charges were brought.

7. EDWARD L. DOHENY
GREYSTONE MANSION, 905 LOMA VISTA DR., BEVERLY HILLS

Oil magnate Edward L. Doheny built this 55-room mansion in 1928 for his son, Edward Lawrence (Ned) Doheny Jr. Just a few months after the younger Doheny moved into the 46,054-square-foot home with his wife and five children, he and his secretary, Hugh Plunkett, were found dead in Doheny's bedroom. Some say the secretary shot Doheny because he was denied a raise, then turned the gun on himself. But published reports at the time suggested Doheny and his secretary were lovers and that Doheny fired both shots because he was afraid his family would find out about his affair. Today Greystone is owned by the city of Beverly Hills.

8. VICKI MORGAN
4171 D COLFAX AVE., STUDIO CITY

Vicki Morgan was the mistress of the late Alfred Bloomingdale, Diners Club founder and member of former President Ronald Reagan's "kitchen cabinet." On July 7, 1983, Morgan was beaten to death with a baseball bat by roommate Marvin Pancoast. He died of AIDS in a prison at Chino in December, 1991.

9. SAL MINEO
8569 HOLLOWAY DR., WEST HOLLYWOOD

After a play rehearsal on the night of Feb. 12, 1976, 37-year-old actor Sal Mineo was stabbed to death after parking his Chevette in the carport of the two-story apartment building. He appeared in the 1955 film "Rebel Without a Cause" with James Dean, Natalie Wood and Nick Adams. All four died unusual or violent deaths. Mineo's killer, 19-year-old pizza deliveryman Lionel Ray Williams, was convicted of second-degree murder, as well as 10 robberies in the neighborhood, and was sentenced to 51 years in prison.

10. ANDREY KUZNETSOV AND VLADIMIR LITVINENKO
8546 W. KNOLL DR., WEST HOLLYWOOD

On the night of Jan. 26, 1992, Russian nationals Andrey Kuznetsov and Vladimir Litvinenko, both 28, were found shot execution-style with their fingertips cut off. Police arrived and found two Russian immigrants ripping the bullets from the bodies, presumably trying to erase any ballistics trail. Serguei Ivanov and Alexander Nikolaev, former members of the Soviet military, were charged in the case. The motive is still unclear.

11. JOHN BELUSHI
8221 SUNSET BLVD., WEST HOLLYWOOD

The exclusive residential hotel, Chateau Marmont, was once the residence of Jean Harlow, Greta Garbo and Errol Flynn. It is also where 33-year-old comedian John Belushi was found dead of a drug overdose in Bungalow No. 2 on March 5, 1982. Belushi's friend, one-time heroin addict and backup vocalist Cathy Smith, was arrested for administering the fatal mixture of cocaine and heroine. She pleaded no contest to a charge of involuntary manslaughter and was sentenced to three years in prison.

12. LENO AND ROSEMARY LABIANCA
3301 WAVERLY, LOS FELIZ

One night after the Sharon Tate murders, and a few miles east of the Tate home, members of the Manson family cult tied up wealthy grocery store owners Leno and Rosemary LaBianca with lamp cords and stabbed them to death in their home. "DEATH TO PIGS" and the misspelled title of a Beatles' song, "HEALTER SKELTER," were written in their blood on a wall and the refrigerator. A carving fork was protruding from Leno's stomach, and the word "WAR" was cut in his flesh.

Manson and three of his followers were convicted of first-degree murder. They were sentenced to die in the gas chamber, but when California abolished the death penalty the next year, their sentences were commuted to life imprisonment. Manson has come up for parole every seven years, but Sharon Tate's sister, Patti, has successfully led campaigns to keep him behind bars.

13. HILLSIDE STRANGLER
703 E. COLORADO ST., GLENDALE

Angelo Buono, a Glendale auto upholsterer, was convicted of sexually torturing and murdering nine women whose bodies were dumped on Los Angeles-area hillsides in 1977 and 1978. Buono's accomplice and cousin, Kenneth Bianchi, in a plea bargain, admitted to five killings. Buono was sentenced to life in prison; Bianchi will be eligible for parole in 2005. Bianchi claimed that most of the murders were committed at this address, Buono's upholstery shop, now a used-car dealership.

14. MICKEY AND TRUDY THOMPSON
53 WOODLYN LANE, BRADBURY

Millionaire racing promoter and pioneering speedster Mickey Thompson and his wife, Trudy, were ambushed and shot to death in the driveway of their walled foothill estate while leaving for work on March 16, 1988. The still-unsolved shootings were thought to be contract killings.

Richard Ramirez, the Night Stalker, displaying palm inked with pentagram sometimes associated with Satanism.

Tony Barnard / Los Angeles Times

15. OTTO SANHUBER AND WALBURGA OESTERREICH
800 BLOCK, LAFAYETTE PARK PLACE, LOS ANGELES

One of the city's most bizarre love affairs was between Oesterreich, the wife of an apron manufacturer, and Sanhuber, a tiny, quiet man who, unknown to Oesterreich's husband, lived for years in the attic over the couple's bed. But on Aug. 22, 1922, Sanhuber came out of his hideaway when he heard Oesterreich and her husband quarrel. Sanhuber shot Fred Oesterreich to death. Walburga Oesterreich was acquitted in 1930. Sanhuber was convicted of manslaughter but was released because of a three-year statute of limitations. The frame house is on a hill overlooking Sunset Boulevard.

16. BONAVENTURE HOTEL
5TH AND FLOWER STREETS, LOS ANGELES

On Oct. 7, 1979, in a room at the downtown luxury hotel, a North Hollywood couple, Eli and Esther Ruven, were shot with a silencer-equipped .22-caliber pistol by alleged Israeli Mafia members Joseph Zakaria and Jehuda Avital in retaliation for a drug deal gone bad. Their bodies were then dismembered and packed into suitcases, which were later thrown into trash dumpsters in Van Nuys and Sherman Oaks. Avital is serving a life sentence without possibility of parole for first-degree murder of Esther and second-degree murder of her husband. Zakaria pleaded guilty to two counts of voluntary manslaughter and two counts of mutilation.

17. NIGHT STALKER
3727 E. HUBBARD ST., EAST LOS ANGELES

After seven months of slipping through unlocked doors and windows before dawn to attack his victims as they slept, Richard Ramirez, the notorious Night Stalker, was captured across the street from this house by as many as 20 neighbors on Aug. 31, 1985. Ramirez was convicted of 13 brutal slayings and 30 related felonies.

18. BLACK DAHLIA
ONCE-VACANT LOT ON NORTON AVENUE SOUTH OF COLISEUM STREET IN THE CRENSHAW DISTRICT

An aspiring 22-year-old actress named Elizabeth Ann Short was tortured and strangled; her body, severed at the waist, was found on Jan. 15, 1947, in a vacant lot. Her organs had been removed, her body drained of blood and an ear-to-ear grin carved on her face. She was nicknamed the Black Dahlia because of her tight-fitting black dresses and her bouffant black hair. The case was never solved.

SOURCES: "Chronicles of L.A. Crime and Mystery: Fallen Angels" by Marvin J. Wolf and Katherine Mader, and "This Is Hollywood: An Unusual Movieland Guide" by Ken Schessler.

Down Rock 'n' Roll's Memory Lane

Some rock stars were born in L.A., others died here. Some came here to record, others just to hang out.

----

1. ALTA CIENEGA MOTEL
1005 N. LA CIENEGA BLVD., ROOM 32, WEST HOLLYWOOD

On the second floor, Navy brat Jim Morrison of The Doors lived off and on in a $10-a-night room in 1969. Located across the street from the Doors' business office, at 8512 Santa Monica Blvd., and just blocks from the Sunset Strip, the Alta Cienega was convenient for Morrison, who had no car, his license having been revoked for drunk driving. The Doors came to be considered one of L.A.'s quintessential bands, although Morrison, one of rock's most magnetic figures, was only 27 when he died in Paris.

2. BILLBOARD LIVE
9039 SUNSET BLVD., WEST HOLLYWOOD

The three-level club with live venue, dance club and upscale supper club was due to open on the site formerly occupied by Gazzarri's. It was at Gazzarri's that famed musical acts such as the Doors, the Byrds, Tina Turner, Guns N' Roses, Van Halen, Sonny & Cher, Poison and Motley Crue launched their careers. During the 1966 Sunset Strip Riots, a summer-long simmering tension among longhairs, police and shop owners, Gazzarri's led the fight to keep all the rock clubs open. In 1949, when the nightclub was known as Sherry's, gangster Mickey Cohen, the West Coast's legendary chieftain, was exiting the club at 4 a.m. with his entourage, when gunmen opened fire, wounding Cohen and killing one of his henchmen.

3. WHISKY A GO GO
SUNSET AND SAN VICENTE BOULEVARDS, WEST HOLLYWOOD

Hollywood's most famous nightclub has served as a nationally recognized showcase for hard rock, soul and blues artists since it opened on Jan. 11, 1963.

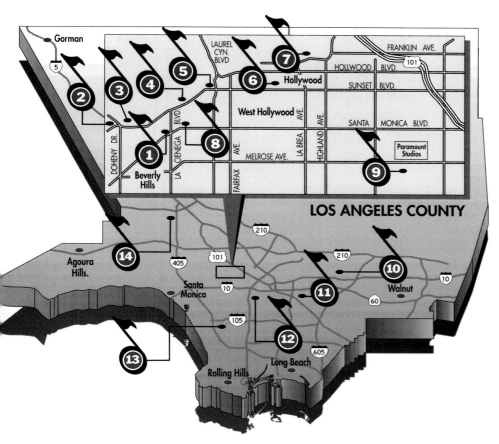

4. HYATT ON SUNSET HOTEL
8401 SUNSET BLVD., WEST HOLLYWOOD

This is the infamous hotel where Led Zeppelin rented as many as six floors, had wild parties and raced motorcycles down hallways. The Who preferred to sling television sets out the windows when they stayed here. Jim Morrison also lived here for a time, until management kicked him out for hanging by his fingertips out a window. The hotel was unofficially dubbed "The Riot House."

5. CHATEAU MARMONT
8221 SUNSET BLVD., HOLLYWOOD

The exclusive residential hotel standing at the head of the famous "Strip" has been a favorite of movie stars and rock personalities: Bob Dylan, Mick Jagger, Ringo Starr, Jefferson Airplane, John Lennon and Yoko Ono. Led Zeppelin rented the bungalows for parties; and comedian John Belushi was found dead of a drug overdose in Bungalow No. 2 on March 5, 1982.

Barney's Beanery, a West Hollywood diner, was a hangout for rockers like Janis Joplin and Jim Morrison.

Cassy Cohen / Los Angeles Times

6. GARDNER ELEMENTARY STREET SCHOOL
7450 HAWTHORNE AVE., HOLLYWOOD

Singer Michael Jackson attended school here in the early 1970s. The school honored Jackson in October, 1989, by naming its auditorium after him.

7. HIGHLAND GARDENS (formerly the Landmark Hotel)
7047 FRANKLIN AVE., ROOM 105, HOLLYWOOD

She was often loud, often coarse, sometimes vulgar, but singer Janis Joplin's blend of bravado and helplessness captivated audiences. Joplin, 27, whose first big hit was "Me and Bobby McGee," died Oct. 4, 1970, of a drug overdose in her hotel room, only a few blocks from the Hollywood Bowl. The Grateful Dead played at her funeral, which was attended by 200 guests who received invitations reading: "Drinks are on Pearl."

8. BARNEY'S BEANERY
8447 SANTA MONICA BLVD., WEST HOLLYWOOD

The old-time diner, long a hangout for rock personalities like Janis Joplin and Jim Morrison, was featured in a drawing on Joplin's album "I Got Dem Ol Kosmic Blues Again, Mama." Legend has it that Joplin hit Morrison over the head with a Southern Comfort bottle here, yet others believe it occurred at a party at John Davidson's house in the Hollywood Hills.

9. LUCY'S EL ADOBE
5536 MELROSE AVE., HOLLYWOOD

Located on a rather seedy stretch of Melrose across from Paramount Studios, this eatery opened in 1964 and was an instant success, drawing customers from the worlds of politics and entertainment. By the late 1970s, almost every Elektra/Asylum artist was a regular there. Songwriter Jimmy Webb ran up two years of meal tabs before hitting it big with songs such as "MacArthur Park" and "Up, Up and Away." It was here that Linda Ronstadt was introduced to then California Gov. Edmund G. (Jerry) Brown Jr., sparking a lengthy romance.

10. EL MONTE LEGION STADIUM
11151 VALLEY BLVD., EL MONTE

The colorful pink building was a popular place for teen-agers during the 1950s. Big-name entertainers flocked to the hall for concerts—among them Chuck Berry, Johnny Otis, Ray Charles, Fats Domino, Ike and Tina Turner, Little Stevie Wonder and L.A.'s first integrated pop group, the Jaguars. Later, Art Laboe brought his Oldies but Goodies Show to the Legion. The 160,000-square-foot stadium, built in 1927, gave way to a post office in 1974.

11. GOLDEN GATE THEATER
ATLANTIC AND WHITTIER BOULEVARDS, EAST LOS ANGELES

East L.A.'s most famous bands—Thee Midniters, Cannibal and the Head-hunters and the Jaguars—played here. The 1960s Midniters' song "Whittier Boulevard" was particularly popular among Saturday night cruisers.

12. 'LOUIE, LOUIE' BIRTHPLACE
WEST 54TH STREET, LOS ANGELES

It was in this house in 1955 that Richard Berry wrote the song "Louie, Louie," the garage-rock classic with calypso-flavor about a homesick Jamaican sailor talking to a bartender named Louie. Richard Berry and the Pharaohs sold about 130,000 copies on Flip Records in 1957, but eight years later, the Kingsmen turned it into a

Golden Gate Theater, where East L.A.'s most famous bands played.

Mike Meadows / Los Angeles Times

The Onion, a center for counterculture antics and political protests in the '60s.

Michael Edwards / Los Angeles Times

smash hit. Berry grew up in South-Central Los Angeles and attended Thomas Jefferson High School.

13. HAWTHORNE HIGH SCHOOL
4859 EL SEGUNDO BLVD., HAWTHORNE

The Beach Boys' musical career began at Hawthorne High School in 1961, when Brian Wilson, his younger brothers, Carl and Dennis, high school chum Al Jardine and cousin, Mike Love (who attended nearby Dorsey High), decided to form a band. For almost three decades, the band has generated a mystical vision of California coastal life through its sun-drenched tunes. Brian Wilson reportedly was inspired to write the song "Fun, Fun, Fun" when he saw a girl driving by in her daddy's T-Bird as he stood at the Foster's Freeze, 11969 Hawthorne Blvd.

14. THE ONION
9550 HASKELL AVE., SEPULVEDA

In February, 1966, the Grateful Dead played at this San Fernando Valley church as part of the "Acid Test" series organized by the Merry Pranksters, a group of Bay Area hippies dedicated to spreading the gospel of freedom and drug use. The event came just a few months before the psychedelic drug LSD was outlawed. Called the Onion because of its distinctive architecture, the Valley Unitarian Church was a center for political protests in the 1960s. Today, it is known as the Sepulveda Unitarian Universalist Society.

■ **More about the Merry Pranksters, see next page.**

SOURCE: "L.A. Musical History Tour" by Art Fein.

The Pranksters'
1939
International
Harvester bus,
painted in a style
that would come
to be called
psychedelic.

Los Angeles Times

Merrily Tripping Back to the '60s

Ride along with us to three Los Angeles bus stops, the sites of seminal events of the 1960s. These are the places—now unremarkable and as yet unmarked—where countercultural pioneers like the Grateful Dead played and author Ken Kesey's LSD-fueled Merry Pranksters gave new meaning to the phrase "acid test."

The Pranksters arrived from Northern California in early February, 1966, temporarily without leader Kesey, author of "One Flew Over the Cuckoo's Nest" (1962) and "Sometimes a Great Notion" (1964). In attempting to avoid arrest on marijuana possession charges, he had first faked a suicide attempt, then fled to Mexico.

The Pranksters followed him in their 1939 International Harvester school bus, which they called Furthur or, in other moods, Further. The sides of the bus screamed with swirls of bright paint, a style soon to be called psychedelic. The back sported a deck with a Harley Davidson. A sign on the front bumper bore the warning "Caution Weird Load." There was always a chemical larder stocked with LSD—then legal—and marijuana—very illegal—and an intricate sound system that could broadcast and record whatever interesting decibels happened by.

The most joyful noises were those generated by the Grateful Dead, whose earliest concert tours were the soundtrack for the Pranksters' odyssey.

The entourage's Los Angeles pilgrimage—with 14 people dressed in bizarre clothes—stopped first at the Sepulveda Unitarian Universalist Society's bulbous wooden sanctuary, nicknamed "the Onion" because of its distinctive architecture. The Pranksters had a friend there, the Rev. Paul Sawyer, a Unitarian minister who invited the group to party at his church. The next day, under the watchful eyes of passers-by, the group headed toward Compton for what would become known as the "Electric Kool-Aid Acid Test," just a few months before LSD was outlawed.

At the wheel was Neal Cassady—the model for Dean Moriarty, the character in Jack Kerouac's Beat literary classic, "On the Road"—who a short time later would die in Mexico from exposure to the cold.

While L.A. was still smoldering from the Watts riots six months earlier, helmeted police set up wooden sawhorses to cordon off the area around an automotive repair garage at 13331 S. Alameda St. The Pranksters were inside lining 30-gallon trash cans, filling them with Kool-Aid and pouring in a couple of glass ampoules of pure LSD. They figured that one full Dixie cup equaled 50 micrograms of acid. Since the standard dose was about 300 micrograms, that equaled six Dixie cups. But after many guests downed several glasses, someone recomputed to discover that one cup equaled 300 micrograms.

"Wavy Gravy"—patriarch of another countercultural institution, the Hog Farm—stood by the trash cans all night, saying, "The one on the right is for the kids or kittens, and the one on the left is electric for the tigers."

Prankster Ken Babbs kept repeating into the microphone, "Freak, freak, freak!" and a woman sat in the middle of the floor screaming, "Who cares? Who cares?"

A slide show of flowers and patterns continued through the evening, and a strobe light flashed everywhere. Many of the locals thought the "happening" was just a friendly get-together, until one woman yelled, "It's LSD! It's LSD! My shrink told me never to take it again."

Many of the several hundred guests hit the pay phone to call doctors; others phoned friends with the address.

The last test took place at the Carthay Studios on Pico Boulevard.

This time no acid went into the Kool-Aid, only some dry ice for a bubbling effect. However, many who attended thought they were high.

When the party was over, more than half the Pranksters quietly piled into the bus and took off for Mexico. The ones left behind never quite knew what happened.

The revolution of the LSD-soaked exercises in mass ecstasy collapsed in the late 1960s, with LSD's reputation bloodied by tales of suicides, haunting flashbacks and bad trips.

Some of the Pranksters—once dedicated to spreading the gospel of expanded consciousness through freedom and drug use—now live more material lives as writers, publishers, builders, lawyers. One is a yogurt magnate.

The infamous old bus, Further, rests with its faded paint crinkling on Kesey's 65-acre ranch near Eugene, Ore. And no one knows what happened to Kesey's old familiar sign that once welcomed guests with the greeting, "No Left Turn Unstoned."

R.I.P. in L.A.

'Cemeteries to the Stars' serve as reminders of the city's glamorous past and shrines for legions of devoted fans.

----

1. WESTWOOD MEMORIAL PARK
1218 GLENDON AVE., WESTWOOD

This tiny cemetery is sandwiched between the tall buildings of Westwood, creating a quiet haven in the midst of one of Los Angeles' most urban spots. Despite its postage-stamp size, it is the final resting place of many luminaries. And there is

Marilyn Monroe: Her crypt at Westwood Memorial Park is always marked with fresh flowers.

room for more, at about $13,000 per plot.

Marilyn Monroe's crypt is always marked with fresh flowers. Armand Hammer, the chairman of Occidental Petroleum, was laid to rest alongside family members in a mausoleum behind black ironwork doors with an Egyptian motif.

Others buried here include young actress Heather O'Rourke of "Poltergeist" fame; songwriter Harry Warren, who wrote "You'll Never Know (Just How Much I Love You)"; musician Buddy Rich; Playboy centerfold Dorothy Stratten, and actresses Donna Reed and Natalie Wood. The ashes of actor Peter Lawford were entombed here in 1984 but removed and scattered at sea in 1988.

2. SAN FERNANDO MISSION CEMETERY
1160 STRANWOOD AVE., MISSION HILLS

The cemetery was founded in 1797. One Jose Antonio was listed as its first recorded internment on April 7, 1798. This is the final resting place of William Frawley, best known as Fred Mertz on "I Love Lucy," and William Bendix, "The Life of Riley." The grave that draws the most visitors is that of 17-year-old rocker Ritchie Valens of Pacoima, who died in an Iowa plane crash on Feb. 3, 1959, along with renowned rock-and-roll singers Buddy Holly and J. P. Richardson, "The Big Bopper." A flat marker, No. 248, is inscribed with five notes from Valens' first hit single in September, 1958, "Come On—Let's Go."

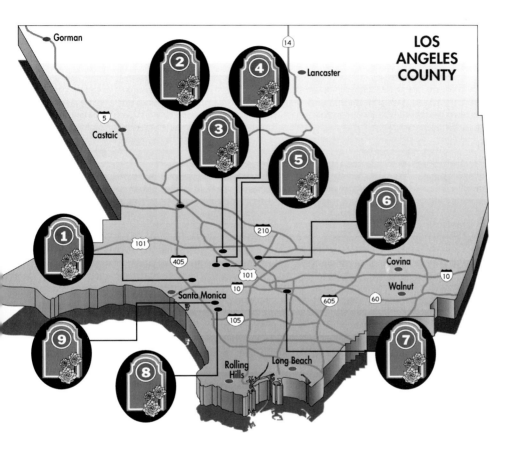

3. FOREST LAWN HOLLYWOOD HILLS
6300 FOREST LAWN DR., BURBANK

This is the second largest of Hubert Eaton's cemetery complexes and is world-famous for its mingling of art and history with the business of undertaking. Near the George Washington monument is the final resting place of comedian Buster Keaton. Among the famous interred here are Stan Laurel, the Liberace family, Forrest Tucker of "F-Troop," Jack Webb—better known as Joe Friday on "Dragnet"—actor Freddie Prinze of "Chico and the Man," singer Andy Gibb, rhythm-and-blues singer Esther Phillips and gospel singer Tony Fontane. Others include Jason Robards Sr., Ernie Kovacs, Godfrey Cambridge, Ozzie Nelson and George Raft.

4. BETH OLAM
900 N. GOWER ST., HOLLYWOOD

The Jewish cemetery adjoins the Hollywood Memorial Cemetery. Its name

Bob Chamberlin / Los Angeles Times

Mel Blanc's famous sign-off, "That's All, Folks," is engraved on a five-foot marble memorial at Beth Olam.

means "House of the World." Hollywood's favorite gangster, Benjamin (Bugsy) Siegel, rests in a mausoleum with a marker that does not mention the nickname he so detested. It has been said that Siegel, who was shot to death by fellow mobsters on June 21, 1947, slept in cold cream and a chin strap because of his secret aspirations to stardom.

Mel Blanc's famous sign-off, "That's All, Folks," is engraved on a five-foot marble memorial to Blanc, the voice of Bugs Bunny, Porky Pig and innumerable other cartoon characters.

5. HOLLYWOOD MEMORIAL CEMETERY
6000 SANTA MONICA BLVD., LOS ANGELES
(BETWEEN GOWER STREET AND VAN NESS AVENUE)

Some of Hollywood's history can be revisited on these 57 palm-studded acres with more than 77,000 graves, crypts, mausoleums and cenotaphs. Among unusual features is the epitaph on the grave of actress Joan Hackett in the Sanctuary of Trust: "Go away, I'm asleep."

Actress Marion Davies, longtime mistress of William Randolph Hearst, is entombed in a handsome white mausoleum with stone cherubs and room for 12; producer-director Cecil B. DeMille is lavishly entombed, purportedly with his feet pointing toward Paramount; Rudolph Valentino's marker almost always bears the lipstick imprint of a kiss; the burial site of Carl (Alfalfa) Switzer of the Our Gang comedies, killed in 1959 in a fight over a $50 debt, is marked with a picture of Petey, the black-eyed Our Gang dog. The most notable landmark is a marble rocket ship, an exact replica of the Pioneer Atlas that went into orbit Dec. 18, 1958. It marks the grave of Carl Morgan Bigsby, a publisher and admirer of the space program.

Others here include Charlie Chaplin Jr., Harry Cohn, Nelson Eddy, Douglas Fairbanks Sr., Peter Finch, Janet Gaynor, Peter Lorre, Tyrone Power, Norma and Constance Talmadge, Clifton Webb and Hollywood pioneer John T. Gower.

6. FOREST LAWN GLENDALE
1712 GLENDALE AVE., GLENDALE

In 1906, founder Hubert Eaton turned a tiny Glendale graveyard into an enormous art-filled memorial park, which later became a multimillion-dollar enterprise. More than a million people visit the Glendale park each year. Since 1929, thousands of couples have exchanged vows in the chapel there, including Ronald Reagan and Jane Wyman on Jan. 26, 1940.

Tom Mix, cowboy star of the silents and early talkies, reportedly was buried with his famous belt buckle that spelled his name in diamond letters. Other celebrities interred here include Alan Ladd, Mary Pickford, W. C. Fields, Humphrey Bogart, Spencer Tracy, Robert Taylor, Walt Disney, Errol Flynn, Clark Gable, Carol Lombard, Jean Harlow, Gracie Allen and Nat King Cole.

■ "Errol Flynn: Hero or Villain?" see Page 44.

7. CALVARY
4201 WHITTIER BLVD., LOS ANGELES

With its colorful, glass-enclosed Stations of the Cross and elaborate columned mausoleums, Calvary is one of the most ornate Roman Catholic cemeteries and the last resting place for some of the wealthiest and most influential church members.

Entombed in a crypt near the chapel altar are Cardinal McIntyre, Archbishop Cantwell and Bishops Conaty, Amat and Mora. Cardinal Manning is buried in a simple grave in the Good Shepherd section.

In a grotto of polished red marble is the tomb of oil tycoon Edward Doheny, who was acquitted in the Teapot Dome scandal a few years before he died in 1935. The family had several mansions and is remembered in Los Angeles with a street and a state beach named in its honor.

Hollywood film legend John Barrymore also has a crypt here, though he's actually buried in the family plot in Philadelphia. Another famous grave is that of Louis Francis Cristillo, better known as Lou Costello.

8. HILLSIDE MEMORIAL PARK
6001 CENTINELA AVE., LOS ANGELES

A six-column marble structure with a stepped waterfall marks the grave of singer Al Jolson. The waterfall, visible from the 405 Freeway, has become a major landmark for the area.

Among other celebrities buried here are David Janssen, Jack Benny, Allan Sherman, Percy Faith, Mickey Cohen, Vic Morrow. Here, too, are George A. Jessel and Eddie Cantor, who wrote his own epitaph: "Here in nature's arms I nestle, free at last from Georgie Jessel."

A six-column marble structure marks the grave of singer Al Jolson at Hillside Memorial Park.

Ken Lubas / Los Angeles Times

9. HOLY CROSS
5835 WEST SLAUSON AVE., CULVER CITY

The most prominent plot in the Grotto at Holy Cross, beneath the statue of a kneeling angel, belongs to Rita Hayworth. Other notables here include Ray Bolger, Bing Crosby, Jimmy Durante, Conrad Hilton Jr., Spike Jones, Bela (Dracula) Lugosi, Sharon Tate Polanski, Mario Lanza, Walter O'Malley, Louella Parsons, Rosalind Russell, Gloria Vanderbilt and her twin sister, Thelma Viscountess Furness.

SOURCE: "Permanent Californians" by Judi Culbertson and Tom Randall.

Errol Flynn: Hero or Villain?

There is nothing there now but a dusty, vacant stretch of weed-studded land high in the Hollywood Hills. But still the star-struck and the curious come.

Once they made the trek up Nichols Canyon to a site just off Mulholland Drive to catch a glimpse of the rambling Connecticut-style farmhouse, designed by screen legend Errol Flynn. The house they could see, but like those who come today, they only could imagine the one-way mirrors in the bedroom ceilings and the listening device in the ladies' room in Flynn's "fortress of bacchanalian amusements."

It wasn't the fact that Flynn slept there that intrigued Old Hollywood, it was with whom. For his many lovers were said to have included leading ladies, other men's wives and a coterie of young ladies still eligible for Girl Scout badges.

It was here that a small group of Flynn's friends pulled off one of Hollywood's most notorious pranks. In 1942, after spending hours at a Sunset Strip bar, drowning their sorrows over the death of friend John Barrymore, three of the mourners bribed the undertaker and headed back to Flynn's house with Barrymore's body. They propped it up in a chair and waited for their host to arrive. Upon seeing the corpse, Flynn screamed and hid in the oleander bush on the patio. He recovered quickly, poured drinks for his friends, but refused to help them return the body.

Such shenanigans were typical of Flynn, whose real life equaled the swashbuckling adventures of his movies. He was born in Tasmania in 1909, his mother from a seafaring family, his father a distinguished marine biologist.

A combination of accident and luck brought him to Hollywood after a film producer spotted him on an Australian beach.

In 1935, his first year at Warner Bros., he did very little except marry French actress Lili Damita. Their marriage staggered through seven years of violent fights and the birth of their son, Sean, who in 1970 disappeared while working as a free-lance photographer in Cambodia.

Flynn stepped into overnight stardom after filming "Captain Blood." Things came easily to him, including trouble and controversy.

Studio boss Jack Warner once said, "To the Walter Mittys of the world he was all the heroes in one magnificent, sexy animal package."

The notorious San Francisco madam, Sally Stanford, said Flynn was "sweet" and a prodigious lover. "He was the only customer I ever had who tested all of the talent, including both shifts, twice."

Flynn's roguish adventures, amorous escapades and bloody barroom brawls brought him into court on more than one occasion.

In November, 1942, at the pinnacle of his career, two teen-age girls accused him of statutory rape. A ponytailed teen-ager, Betty Hansen, sat on the witness stand detailing a night she spent with Flynn.

The second complainant, 16-year-old Peggy Satterlee, charged that Flynn raped her on two consecutive nights on his yacht.

In a moment of high drama, the actor took the stand. A courtroom reporter wrote, "Flynn's eyes were red-speckled, unslept, and his cheeks were chalk. His smile was patent, false. There were strings in his face, taut and extruded. More than anyone else in the courtroom, Flynn knew exactly what was at stake."

As he finished his testimony, both girls were crying hysterically. Men yelled obscenities. The judge and bailiff attempted to "quell a near-riot."

Errol Flynn in one of his famous hero roles, 1938's "Adventures of Robin Hood."

But his defense attorney, Jerry Giesler, had damaging information about both young women. Hansen had made no protest when Flynn locked the bedroom door and Satterlee had had several affairs with married men and one abortion.

In his closing argument, Giesler stressed that the girls were lying to avoid felony charges for abortion and oral copulation. The prosecutor said Flynn had taken advantage of two innocent underage girls. After the jury of nine women and three men deliberated for more than 24 hours, they acquitted him on both charges.

Flynn's career thrived after the verdict, and he soon set sail for Mexico with 17-year-old Nora Eddington, a redhead who sold cigarettes at the Hall of Justice, whom he met during his trial. He married her and fathered two girls, Deirdre and Rory. His second marriage would also last seven years.

In 1950, before his movie-making career began to decline, he married actress Patrice Wymore. A few years after their daughter, Arnella, was born, they separated and remained so until his death in 1959. Flynn died a burned-out wreck at 50, a 17-year-old nymphet at his side. And even death had its familiar consolations: His cronies buried him with six bottles of whiskey.

Before his fortress was torn down in 1988, it was owned by singer Ricky Nelson and singer-songwriter Stuart Hamblen, among others.

Today, the property is vacant and Flynn's memory is preserved only by Flynn Drive and the affection of the occasional film buffs who wander by.

The Hauntings

Haunts of the rich and famous, plus strange tales of psychic phenomena, add mystery to the fantasy capital.

1. PICO ADOBE
10940 SEPULVEDA BLVD., MISSION HILLS

Once owned by Andreas Pico, brother of the last Mexican governor of California, this famous adobe was restored by Pico's illegitimate son, Romulo Pico, and his wife, Caterina, in 1873. Only two adobe walls remained by 1930, when Dr. Mark R. Harrington bought the shell of a building.

During the night, Harrington said, he would hear heels clicking as in a Spanish

The ghost of Caterina Pico has been known to walk the staircase of the Pico Adobe in Mission HIlls.

Mitsu Yasukawa / Los Angeles Times

dance on the downstairs tile floor. The sounds would proceed up the staircase until they were outside his bedroom. The moment he would open the door, the sounds would stop. Harrington staged a seance and said he discovered that Caterina had resumed residency and only wanted to thank him for restoring her old home.

The adobe is owned by the city of Los Angeles and open to the public. Many visitors have said they felt a presence here, and past caretakers have reported unexplained phenomena. But the present-day caretaker insists she has never seen or heard ghosts.

Maybe Caterina got restless and moved on.

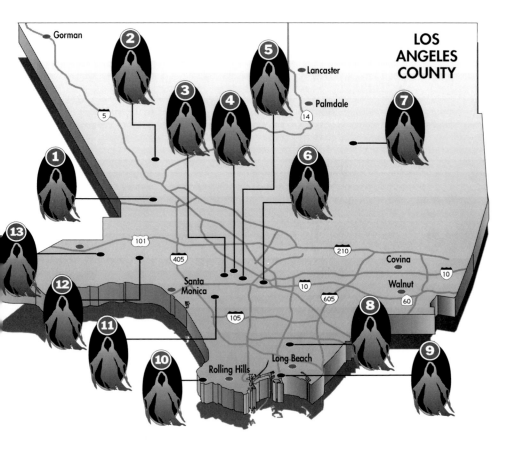

LOS ANGELES COUNTY

Gorman

Lancaster

Palmdale

Santa Monica

Covina

Walnut

Long Beach

Rolling Hills

2. PLUM CANYON
SAUGUS

Plum Canyon, a long, narrow rock crevice in Saugus that runs from Vasquez Canyon to Bouquet Canyon Road, is reportedly where a small contingent of Spanish soldiers was ambushed and slain in 1821 by Native Americans during the war between Spain and Mexico. Repeated stories of Spanish ghosts and strange happenings in the canyon keep the incident alive.

Since the mid-19th century, in a spot a little to the west, between Bouquet and Mint canyons, the ghost of a Spanish woman in a light satin dress and blue shawl has reportedly been spotted floating along the path.

3. THE COMEDY STORE
8433 W. SUNSET BLVD., WEST HOLLYWOOD

Ciro's opened in 1939 and soon became the town's grandest nightspot. It was a place where a jokester dressed as an Arab sheik created a near riot by dropping a bag of phony diamonds on the floor. Today, in a locked and empty room of what is now the Comedy Store, it is said that the murmuring voices of people allegedly bumped off by mobsters can be heard.

4. HOLLYWOOD ROOSEVELT HOTEL
7000 HOLLYWOOD BLVD., HOLLYWOOD

The ghost of actor Montgomery Clift, who died of a heart attack in 1966, is said to roam the ninth floor of this refurbished hotel, built in 1927. Hotel records show that Clift rented Room 928 for about three months in 1952 while filming "From Here to Eternity." Guests, maids and security guards have reported seeing or hearing Clift's ghost playing his trumpet and reciting lines while pacing the hallway.

Marilyn Monroe's reflection has been reported to haunt a mirror that once hung in Suite 1200, often used by the star. The mirror now hangs in the manager's office.

Others have reported seeing a sobbing little girl looking for her mother throughout the hotel, and a man wearing a white suit loitering in the Blossom Room, the ballroom where the first Academy Awards were held in 1929.

Some say they have even heard a voice calling them to the hotel's roof and, once they got there, felt the presence of someone trying to pull them off the rooftop. In 1932, Harry Lee, an out-of-work actor, leaped from the roof to his death.

5. BROWNSTONE APARTMENTS
1168 BELLVIEW AVE., LOS ANGELES

Marion Parker, a 12-year-old twin, was strangled and dismembered in 1927 by a 19-year-old college student named Edward Hickman in his room at the Bellevue Arms, on a site now occupied by the Brownstone Apartments.

Michelle Pelland and Steve Daley, who in 1988 purchased and then sold a house on Wilton Place where Parker grew up, said they believed the girl's ghost lived with them. Many parapsychologists believe ghosts seek places where they were happiest or were attracted to during their earthly lives. Pelland and Daley reported hearing footsteps on the stairs and finding certain objects displaced at times, lights going on and off for no known reason. They said they felt they were sharing space with a benevolent, childlike and non-threatening spirit.

6. ALEXANDRIA HOTEL
501 S. SPRING ST., LOS ANGELES

On the outside, this eight-story, 1906 landmark hotel with its 12-story annex— once a showplace whose guests included U.S. presidents and Hollywood celebrities—struggles to fend off drug dealers and prostitutes. Inside, a ghost appearing to be in her late 30s, wearing the fashions of the era when the hotel was new and ritzy (veiled cartwheel hat and high-necked black dress with bustle), is said to wander the hallways looking for a loved one.

7. BIG ROCK CANYON
EIGHT MILES SOUTHEAST OF PEARBLOSSOM
ON BIG ROCK CANYON ROAD

The legend of Sasquatch, or Bigfoot, dates to Native American myths that

The Hollywood Roosevelt Hotel has the reputation of being the favorite haunt of the stars, among them Montgomery Clift and Marilyn Monroe.

Iris Schneider / Los Angeles Times

The Hollywood Roosevelt ballroom in 1929, the year of the first Academy Awards. A ghostly chap wearing a white suit has been spotted loitering in the room.

linked it to "shiny silver moons," which some Bigfoot fans believe means alien spaceships. Whether the creature is a visitor from another planet, a throwback to primitive man or a figment of modern imaginations, there have been a number of reported Bigfoot sightings in the Antelope Valley since the early 1970s.

In 1973, three young men said they saw an 11-foot, apelike creature jump out of the bushes near Sycamore Flats campground and chase them to their truck. They returned to the site after informing the sheriff's office in Lancaster and found hundreds of three-toed prints, some of which were preserved in plaster of Paris. Other Bigfoot tracks are reputedly five-toed.

The Queen Mary is reputed to host a number of supernatural guests at its dock in Long Beach.

The Queen Mary's swimming pool, where some report having seen a spectral, middle-aged woman in an old-fashioned bathing suit taking a plunge.

Six months later, something that appeared to have a 12-foot stride left what looked like 21-inch footprints at South Fork campground. More reports trickled in over the years, including a sighting by two girls on horseback of an "apelike monster" at Devil's Punchbowl County Park, just west of Big Rock Canyon.

8. RANCHO LOS CERRITOS
4600 VIRGINIA ROAD, LONG BEACH

This colonial two-story adobe, built in 1844, was once home to pioneer John Temple. The museum's former curator, Keith Foster, remembers the night several years ago when a group of local curators held a seance at the adobe. The medium summoned up the spirit of Temple, which reportedly lifted a 200-pound library table about six inches off the floor and pinned Foster against the library's glass doors. Foster believes Temple's frustrated spirit assumed Foster knew where Temple had buried silver treasure on the grounds. No one has ever found the treasure.

9. QUEEN MARY
PIER J, AT THE END OF CALIFORNIA 710, LONG BEACH

The old 390-stateroom liner, now a major tourist attraction, was known as the "Gray Ghost" during World War II because her huge form was seen appearing and quickly vanishing through fog. She is also said to be home to a number of ghosts.

Many unexplained happenings have been reported near the ship's swimming pool, in the morgue, in the engine room and in one of the kitchens. Among these were reports of a middle-aged woman in an old-fashioned bathing suit diving into an empty basin. (According to ship's records, several people drowned in the pool during its 31 years of service.)

Other reports include sightings of an elegantly dressed "Woman in White" draped over the piano in the Queen's Salon and dancing by herself in the shadows; of Senior 2nd Officer W.E. Stark, who died on board in 1949 after accidentally drinking acid; and of a miniskirted young woman pacing around the pool and disappearing behind a pillar.

And there have been strange sightings in the ship's galley, where a cook was said to have been thrown into a heated oven during a wartime brawl. Some have reported lights going on and off by themselves, utensils disappearing, dishes moving about and a stranger entering and then vanishing.

Only a few of the ship's resident ghosts have ever been identified. The incidents that bind them to the ship—whether truth or fiction—are mostly lost to history.

10. POINT VICENTE LIGHTHOUSE
RANCHO PALOS VERDES

The white stucco lighthouse with its red tile roof—which stands in relative isolation on a point of land—has warned ships away from the dangerous peninsula cliffs since 1926 and was a key lighthouse and communications station during World War II.

Its lore includes a female ghost in a flowing gown seen walking nearby. Legend has it that she is searching for a lover lost in a shipwreck. Skeptics claim the apparition was created by an unusual reflection from the rotation of the lighthouse lamp.

11. CULVER STUDIOS
9336 WASHINGTON BLVD., CULVER CITY

In 1924, pioneer filmmaker Thomas Ince died mysteriously while celebrating his 43rd birthday aboard William Randolph Hearst's yacht. Legend has it that Hearst caught his mistress, Marion Davies, kissing Charlie Chaplin and shot at Chaplin, accidentally killing Ince.

Pt. Vicente Lighthouse looking out toward Catalina Island. A female ghost has been reported nearby, searching for a shipwrecked lover.

Ken Lubas / Los Angeles Times

Rumors of hauntings have persisted at this 76-year-old studio, built by Ince. They include a 1988 report from two carpenters who said they saw a man in a bowler hat on a catwalk who told them, "I don't like what you're doing to my studio," before disappearing through a wall.

12. JOAN CRAWFORD'S HOUSE
426 N. BRISTOL AVE., BRENTWOOD

Actress Joan Crawford purchased this home, which she named "El Jordo," just before her marriage in 1928 to actor Douglas Fairbanks Jr. Sometime during the 1940s, she removed all the bathtubs because she regarded sitting in bath water unsanitary. Her daughter Christina, in her 1978 book, "Mommie Dearest," told of growing up in this house in a nightmare of alcoholism, abuse and terror.

The current owners hired a minister from the Healing Light Church to perform an exorcism of the house. Nevertheless, the owners say the ghosts of a caretaker and a dog eluded the exorcist and remain there.

13. LEONIS ADOBE
23537 CALABASAS ROAD, CALABASAS

In 1878, Don Miguel Leonis, a powerful Basque immigrant feared and hated for the dictatorial way he controlled his massive ranch, moved to this house with his Indian wife, Espiritu. After Leonis' death in a wagon accident in 1889, rumors about murder began to spread, but nothing was ever proved. Espiritu held on to the ranch until her death in 1906. Later it was sold to a couple named Agoure—from whom the town of Agoura got its name.

New owners reported hearing the sound of heavy footsteps upstairs at times when the only people known to be in the house were downstairs. Doors are reported to have shut by themselves. Visitors said they have seen ghostly forms and heard crying, while residents reported hearing the heavy slamming of things and footsteps above the dining room. Back in the 1930s a woman living in the house reported that she was leaning on a second-floor porch railing, heard a creaking sound, then felt hands grip her shoulders and pull her back. The next day an inspection revealed rotted railing. Had she leaned a tiny bit farther, the woman insisted, the railing would have broken.

SOURCES: "Hollywood Haunted: A Ghostly Tour of Filmland" by Laurie Jacobson and Marc Wanamaker; "This Is Hollywood, An Unusual Movieland Guide" by Ken Schessler; "Mysterious California, Strange Places and Eerie Phenomena in the Golden State" by Mike Marinacci; "Fallen Angels" by Marvin J. Wolfe and Katherine Mader; "The Ghostly Register" by Arthur Myers, and Times files.

II.
ETHNIC, ECLECTIC
AND ECCENTRIC

We tend to think of L.A. as perpetually new, endlessly revamping itself on the trendy frontier. But the City of Angels (stage whisper, please) actually has a past—sometimes noble, sometimes tawdry, but always vibrant and theatrical.

These pages trace that past to the Native Americans who roamed the Basin before Spanish conquerors and disease virtually wiped them out. Only vestiges of those indigenous pre-Angelenos survive (in words like "Malibu," from the Chumash language, meaning "the surf sounds loud"). But with Curbside's help, you can unearth traces of ancient burial grounds in the shadows of modern skyscrapers.

Spanish and Mexican settlers, of course, established El Pueblo de Nuestra Senora La Reina de Los Angeles. Southern California's colonial heritage is rich and pervasive, yet often hidden from tourist haunts. From historic adobes to buried doubloons, you'll find pointers here (sorry, the treasure map is a bit vague).

And there are other ethnic roots to explore—African-American communities in the Santa Clarita Valley as well as South Central, and a Jewish settlement in Boyle Heights, with a cemetery in Chavez Ravine a century before the Dodgers came west.

L.A.'s yesterdays are replete with indelible tales and names writ large—including evangelist Aimee Semple McPherson, whose out-of-pulpit escapades made tabloid headlines from the Jazz Age to World War II; the Zoot Suit riots; Col. Griffith Jenkins Griffith, would-be wife-murderer and civic philanthropist; and little Kathy Fiscus, whose failed rescue launched local TV news.

Along this colorful path, Curbside stops to admire architectural oddities (a Southland trademark), WPA monuments and offbeat museums and libraries.

Ancient Burial Grounds

Centuries ago, Native Americans roamed the L.A. Basin. Parks, businesses and schools sit atop burial grounds.

---

1. MALIBU

For 5,000 years—long before Annette Funicello and Frankie Avalon portrayed Malibu as the world's premier surfing colony—this area was the home of the Chumash. On Oct. 10, 1542, Juan Rodriguez Cabrillo, the first Spanish explorer of Alta California, stopped at a village on the site of what is now Malibu Lagoon State Beach. To greet Cabrillo's two ships the villagers rode into the surf with their swift, red-planked canoes, which so impressed the conquistador that he named the village Pueblo de las Canoas.

The Chumash, however, called their lagoon village Humaliwu, meaning "the surf sounds loud." After Cabrillo departed, Humaliwu continued its peaceful existence for more than 200 years.

Nearby, at Cypress Cove, not far from the homes of Mel Gibson, Emilio Estevez and other Hollywood notables, the remains of six Chumash were unearthed in 1991 during construction of three homes. The remains were apparently reburied by the developer in cardboard

Archeologists and their assistants work to remove skeletons uncovered by bulldozers at a construction site near Point Dume in 1969.

George R. Fry / Los Angeles Times

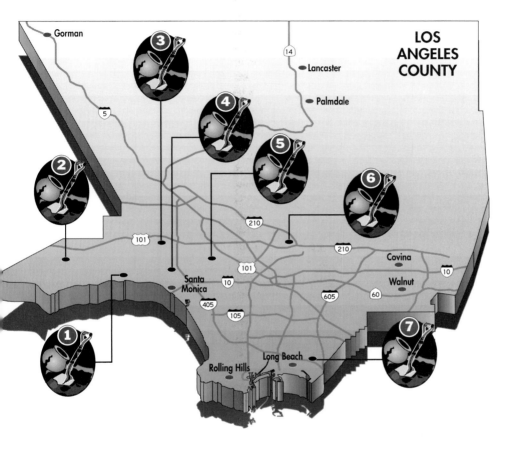

boxes and plastic bags, but not in accordance with Chumash tradition or state regulations, which require crews to stop work and notify the county coroner when remains are discovered, followed by reburial of the remains according to tribal ritual. The developer later reported to the state that he reburied the remains properly.

Farther north, at a Point Dume trailer park project, more remains were uncovered in April, 1969.

2. MALIBU CREEK STATE PARK
1925 LAS VIRGENES RD., CALABASAS

In the northeast corner of the park sat the Chumash village of Talepop. The village existed roughly from the year 1000 to the early 1800s. Talepop sat between territories thought to have been inhabited by the Chumash and Gabrielinos. Although tribe members often intermarried, the dead usually were buried according to their own tribal customs.

Digging up Lost
Village of Encino,
Ventura
Boulevard and
Balboa Avenue,
in 1985.

Joel P. Lugavere / Los Angeles Times

In 1987, the remains of what are thought to be a Gabrielino woman and child were unearthed by a construction worker digging a sewer trench. The two bodies had been cremated in the pit where they were buried with manzanita berries, apparently a food offering.

Entrance to the park and a small museum at the visitors center is on Las Virgenes Road just south of Mulholland Highway. The park is open 8 a.m. to 5 p.m. daily and the visitors center is open on weekends and holidays only.

3. LOST VILLAGE OF ENCINO
LOS ENCINOS STATE HISTORIC PARK,
16756 MOORPARK ST., ENCINO

A large settlement is described in the 1769 diary of Franciscan missionary Juan Crespi, a member of the Gaspar de Portola scouting group. Crespi wrote about visiting a village with a spring-fed pool in the area that is now the state park.

In 1984, across the street from the park, more than 2 million artifacts—from stone tools to arrowheads and beads—were accidentally unearthed by a construction crew, along with remains of about 20 inhabitants of a 3,000-year-old Gabrielino village.

An archeologist catalogued the artifacts. Some were delivered to two mission museums; others were sent to the state-run museum in the park near the site. Park rangers give free tours of the grounds from 1 to 4 p.m. Wednesday through Sunday.

4. UNIVERSITY HIGH SCHOOL
WEST LOS ANGELES

Explorer Portola camped at the village on the site known as Kurovongna, meaning "a place in the sun," on Aug. 4, 1769, traveling the route that became known as El Camino Real; the missionary Padre Junipero Serra is also believed to have said Mass here. Construction of University High School in 1925 unearthed evidence of the village. In 1975, a science teacher and students from the school dug up more artifacts and some bones from what archeologists now believe is an Indian burial site. The springs still flow at the school.

5. LA BREA TAR PITS
GEORGE C. PAGE MUSEUM, 5801 WILSHIRE BLVD., LOS ANGELES

Nothing can top the spectacle of sticky black asphalt oozing out of the ground in the middle of one of the country's largest cities, spitting out some of North America's oldest bones.

For millennia, humans have excavated the surface tar. The Indians who lived in the area used it to waterproof their boats and reed huts, to attach abalone fishhooks to sinew fishing lines, to glue ornaments onto pots and baskets and to repair broken implements, transporting the material along the ancient Indian path today known as Wilshire Boulevard.

■ **For more about La Brea Tar Pits, see below.**

6. SHELDON RESERVOIR
PASADENA

Centuries ago, the Arroyo Seco was known by the Gabrielinos as Hahamongna, meaning "fruitful valley, flowing waters." In 1938, when Pasadena city workers began digging in the Arroyo Seco to build the Sheldon Reservoir, remains of 53 ancient people were found.

7. CAL STATE LONG BEACH
1250 BELLFLOWER BLVD., LONG BEACH

Archeologists theorize that the Gabrielino village of Puvungna moved over the years, setting up camp at various sites on the hill now occupied by Cal State Long Beach. As the villagers' huts of woven reeds over sapling frames wore out, they built new ones nearby. Puvungna was the birthplace of a deity called Chunquichnish, the Gabrielinos' lawgiver and god, who was sometimes venerated in ceremonies using a hallucinogenic concoction of jimson weed.

In 1972, workers digging a water trench uncovered a burial site that led to the discovery of Puvungna. It took the university six years to rebury the remains. Puvungna is listed on the National Register of Historic Places, but when officials drew up plans to develop a 22-acre strip of land on the western edge of the campus, they apparently made no mention of its historical status. A court halted construction, and the university is awaiting a decision on its appeal of the stalled expansion plans.

La Brea Tar Pits

Sitting in the heart of the Mid-Wilshire district, alongside towering office buildings and crowded streets, is an attraction that no other U.S. city can boast: a graveyard for saber-toothed cats, dire wolves, imperial mammoths and Los Angeles' first known murder victim.

Since the turn of the century, more than 3 million fossils have been discovered in the muck and ooze of the La Brea Tar Pits, a 23-acre site near Wilshire Boulevard and Fairfax Avenue. The site today includes a museum and viewing area. But back in the early 1900s, it was better known for something else that lay beneath the soil—oil.

In the 1860s, Rancho La Brea was purchased for $2.50 an acre by Maj. Henry Hancock and his brother John, who quarried asphalt and shipped it to San Francisco to pave the city's streets. After the quarry was abandoned, water gradually filled the area, creating a small lagoon.

Thousands of tar-soaked bones, considered a curiosity and a nuisance, were first recognized as fossils by William Denton, a friend of the Hancocks, in 1875. But it was not until 1899 that William Orcutt, an engineering and geology graduate of Stanford University working for Union Oil (now Unocal Corp.), began removing and researching fossils in the La Brea Tar Pits. Some bones were identified as belonging to the extinct saber-toothed tiger, dire wolf and giant sloth.

From 1901 to 1905, as oil drilling at the site began, further scientific excavations were conducted by John C. Merriam of UC Berkeley and his students, who uncovered and identified the skeletal remains.

In 1913, Navy Capt. George Allen Hancock, Henry's son, allowed Los Angeles County to excavate the site for two years. During this time, more than 750,000 bones were unearthed and hundreds of oil wells were erected. In 1915, Hancock deeded the 23-acre rancho to the county for excavations and research.

Only one human skeleton has been found, a 25-year-old Indian woman who died 9,000 years ago alongside her pet dog. Believed by the museum to be Los Angeles' first known murder victim, she had her skull crushed by a blunt object, possibly a grinding stone.

In 1972, George C. Page, a local industrialist and philanthropist, offered to build a museum that would house the fossils and where visitors could learn the history of one of the greatest concentrations of prehistoric remains in the world.

In 1975, while the museum's foundation was being dug, workers discovered, for the first time, entire animals that had been trapped in the tar when they came to drink from a nearby stream.

Today, life-size fiberglass models of imperial mammoths stand on the edge of the pool, posed in a struggle to escape the tar beneath the water. The area, a major source of oil and gas in the century's early decades, now supports only a few producing wells. Nearly 3 million fossils have been excavated from the site over the last 90 years.

Rancho La Brea in early part of the century. Oil field is in background.

Security Pacific Collection

Pioneer Cemeteries

These old resting places have a natural ambience often missing in modern manicured parks.

----

1. SAN FERNANDO PIONEER MEMORIAL CEMETERY
BLEDSOE STREET AND FOOTHILL BOULEVARD, SYLMAR

Originally part of the lands of the nearby San Fernando Mission, the cemetery lost its church affiliation more than 150 years ago. It was passed from owner to owner until 1961, when it was donated to the Native Daughters of the Golden West. Records indicate that burials continued until 1939. The 750 graves include Native Americans, Civil War veterans, children who died in the 1918 worldwide influenza epidemic and victims of the 1928 St. Francis Dam disaster. Tours: (818) 367-7957.

2. SAVANNAH MEMORIAL PARK
9263 VALLEY BLVD., ROSEMEAD

Before the Civil War, many Southern families settled in El Monte, then called Lexington. Next door, on slightly higher ground, stood the community of Savannah. The elevated land made it the choice as the burial site for residents of swampy Lexington. The first known burial was in 1846, five years before most of the settlers arrived. Today the privately owned 5 1/2-acre cemetery, with 200 plots remaining of its original 3,000, is run by the El Monte Cemetery Assn. In the 1920s, when the city began to widen Valley Boulevard, construction crews unearthed dozens of corpses outside the cemetery fence. Most of the skeletons were reburied in a mass grave inside the cemetery, but some had deteriorated so much that workers left them untouched and simply paved over them.

3. SIERRA MADRE CEMETERY
553 SIERRA MADRE BLVD., SIERRA MADRE

Atop a choice hillside is a cemetery where 12 of Sierra Madre's 17 original settlers are buried. It was founded in 1884 on the death of Civil War veteran and pioneer John Richardson. The headstones of Confederate soldiers buried here have all been stolen by souvenir hunters or pranksters. All the burial plots at this privately owned 2.3-acre cemetery are filled, and only two granite niches in its mausoleum remain empty.

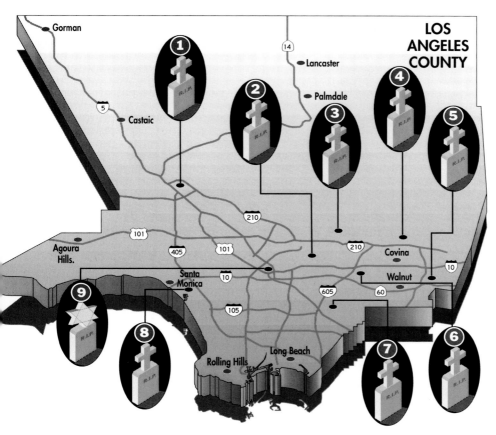

4. FAIRMOUNT CEMETERY
301 N. BALDY VISTA AVE., GLENDORA

Surrounded by a commercial nursery is a tiny, 119-year-old cemetery, begun when settler James Carson Preston donated the two-acre parcel—a former Native American burial site—as a public graveyard. The need arose in 1875 after a German immigrant and woodcutter named Nelson was killed protecting his wood from a thief. Almost 200 other settlers, including potato king J.B. Beardslee, followed Nelson to this graveyard, most under more peaceful circumstances. The Fairmount Cemetery trustees give several tours a year. (818) 335-4440.

5. SPADRA CEMETERY
2882 POMONA BLVD., POMONA

Sandwiched among D.H. Trucking Co., railroad tracks and the Orange Freeway sits a 2 1/2-acre cemetery dating to 1868. Rancher Louis Phillips donated the land as a civic graveyard. Early settlers named the community Spadra after their hometown

Woodlawn Cemetery in Santa Monica was given to the city by the family of an early mayor, Juan Carrillo.

Joe Kennedy / Los Angeles Times

of Spadra Bluff, Ark. In 1971, four years after the last burial, the graveyard was deeded to the Historical Society of Pomona Valley. The cemetery, lined with pepper trees, includes 200 graves. Tours: (909) 623-2198.

6. EL CAMPO SANTO
15415 E. DON JULIAN ROAD, CITY OF INDUSTRY

In the early 1850s, William Workman, who would become one of the founders of Los Angeles' first banking house, set aside an acre of land on his vast rancho for a family cemetery. In 1854, his brother, David, was killed during a cattle drive and became the first family member buried there. In 1917, more than 40 years after the family's bank failed, bankrupting Workman, his grandson, Walter P. Temple Sr., acquired the homestead, having recouped the family fortunes in real estate and oil investments. He had a Greek Revival-style mausoleum built at the entrance to the cemetery, where many members of the family and friends were interred. Also buried here are California's last Mexican governor, Pio Pico, and his wife, Ygnacia. They were originally in another cemetery that the city dismantled in the 1920s. Workman and Pico had been great friends, so the Picos' descendants asked that the couple be moved to the mausoleum. The cemetery is preserved at the six-acre Workman and Temple Homestead, acquired in 1981 by the City of Industry and restored as a cultural landmark. Tours: (818) 968-8492.

7. OLIVE GROVE CEMETERY
10135 S. PAINTER AVE., SANTA FE SPRINGS

Just before the turn of the century, a colony of German Baptists known as Dunkers settled in the area to farm. In 1972, as industry began to move in, the Dunkers moved to Modesto, leaving behind their church and weed-filled graveyard. The Bible Missionary Church, with about 50 members, owns and maintains the cemetery where about 150 pioneering Dunkers and others are buried.

8. WOODLAWN CEMETERY
1847 14TH ST., SANTA MONICA

The picturesque 26.5-acre cemetery at Pico Boulevard and 14th Street served as the burial ground for the family of Juan Carrillo, an early Santa Monica mayor, from 1876 until the family donated the land to Santa Monica in 1898. (310) 450-0781.

9. HOME OF PEACE
LOOKOUT DRIVE AND LILAC TERRACE,
CHAVEZ RAVINE, LOS ANGELES

The cemetery was established in 1855 as the Hebrew Benevolent Society burial grounds in Chavez Ravine, near what is now Dodger Stadium. It's no longer a burial site, but is honored by a plaque on the hillside—"California Registered Landmark No. 822."

At the time rough-and-tumble Los Angeles was home to about 60 Jews who had journeyed from Germany, Austria, Poland and France. As industry grew near downtown, their hilly, three-acre graveyard became surrounded by polluting oil wells and brick kilns. So between 1902 and 1910, all 360 bodies were exhumed and the monuments were moved by horse and wagon to their second resting spot, the current site of Home of Peace in Boyle Heights.

■ **"L.A.'s First Jewish Community," see below.**

L.A.'s First Jewish Community

Jacob Frankfort, 40, believed to be the first Jew to arrive in Los Angeles, had come from Poland in 1841. He was joined by other young Jews from Central Europe who wanted to escape the constraints of life in Germany, Bohemia, Poland and Hungary. They were tough, self-reliant, smart and ambitious.

By 1855, there were 60 Jews living in Los Angeles. Many of them began meeting on Sunday afternoons at the Main Street home of Joseph Newmark, the city's first lay rabbi. This group became Los Angeles' first charity.

It was called the Hebrew Benevolent Society, known as Jewish Family Service. These volunteers provided alms for the town's poor as well as other needy people, sending money to victims of the great Chicago fire of 1871. They attended the sick and even-

View of the Jewish Cemetery in Chavez Ravine before removal began in 1902.

Jewish Historical Society

Los Angeles Times

Today, the site is marked by a small historical plaque.

tually would fund a cemetery.

But first they had to select a location where the dead could truly rest in peace amid the tumult of infant Los Angeles.

For $1, the society purchased a three-acre plot of land from the city in rugged Chavez Ravine. The property, once an Indian village, was where an expedition led by Gaspar de Portola camped on its historic journey from Mexico to Monterey. The land later belonged to Jose Andres Sepulveda and was used for a reservoir.

At the turn of the century, an increasing number of Jews came to Los Angeles, refugees from New York and Chicago seeking better air for their tuberculosis-infected lungs and escape from the garment-industry sweatshops.

Many settled in East Los Angeles because it was a bit cooler and near their downtown businesses. In its heyday, between 1910 and 1950, Boyle Heights was home to between 70,000 and 90,000 Jews. The community built as many as 30 synagogues over the 40-year span.

As the 20th century dawned, the cemetery property had become almost inaccessible, surrounded by oil wells, derricks, brickyards and kilns. The smoke in the area had discolored the shrubbery and blackened the monuments.

By 1902, the Benevolent Society had used the last of the 360 plots, and the more recent dead were buried at the new Home of Peace Cemetery at Whittier Boulevard and Eastern Avenue. Soon all of the original cemetery's remains were moved there.

The society sold part of the old cemetery grounds back to the city, which wasted no time in digging a sewer line for a proposed quarantine house, or "pesthouse," for smallpox sufferers and later for plague victims.

But as the plague waned in the 1930s, the land was abandoned and became a garbage dump.

In 1935, the city donated the site to military planners, who built one of the nation's largest naval reserve armories. Jewish ownership of the remaining graveyard property, except for mineral rights, ended in 1943, when the society deeded it to the government for a housing project that never got off the ground.

Eventually, the U.S. government agreed to sell the land, and it came back to the city yet again. Later the city traded the property to Walter O'Malley, who made it the site of Dodger Stadium.

Today, Jewish Family Service still receives royalties of about $900 a year from its $1 cemetery investment.

Historic Adobes

A scattering of adobe structures with family names and legends that illuminate early chapters of Angeleno history.

----

1. MICHAEL WHITE ADOBE
2701 HUNTINGTON DR., SAN MARINO

In 1845, an English seaman named Michael White built his adobe house on a parcel of land he called Rancho Ysidro. The old adobe stands in the middle of the campus of San Marino High School. The San Marino Historical Society can arrange tours. (818) 568-0119.

■ **San Marino High School site of "Kathy Fiscus Vigil," see Page 70.**

2. EL MOLINO VIEJO
1120 OLD MILL ROAD, SAN MARINO

Originally a mission mill, it became the home of James S. Waite, editor of Los Angeles' first English-language newspaper, the Star, in 1850. It is the Southern California headquarters of the California Historical Society. Open to the public. (818) 449-5450.

3. ORTEGA-VIGARE ADOBE
616 S. RAMONA ST., SAN GABRIEL

This adobe was built by Don Juan Vigare, a soldier of the mission guard, between 1792 and 1805. In the 1860s the house was used as San Gabriel's first bakery. Vigare's great-granddaughter lived here until the 1930s. Today, it is a private residence and not open to the public.

4. RANCHO LAS TUNAS
315 ORANGE ST., SAN GABRIEL

Built in 1776, the same year as the San Gabriel Mission church, it housed the padres who supervised the Indians constructing the mission. After the padres moved into the newly built mission, the adobe became the headquarters for the mission's famous botanical gardens surrounded by cactus. Underground passages allegedly ran from the mission to the adobe's wine cellar. The mission is a private residence and not open to the public.

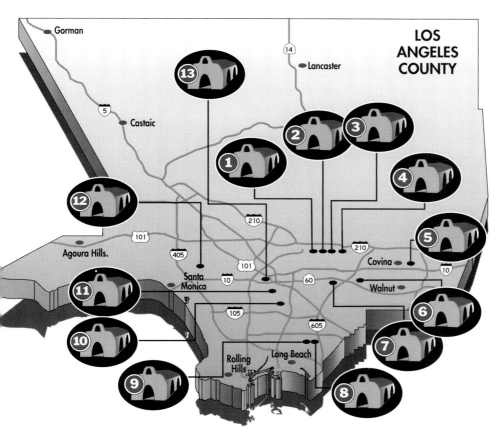

5. LA CASA PRIMERA
1569 N. PARK AVE., POMONA

Built in 1837 by Ygnacio Palomares, a cattle rancher, this five-room adobe is the oldest house in the Pomona Valley. It is the home of the Historical Society of Pomona Valley. A short distance away stands a second home known as El Adobe de Palomares. Open to the public. (909) 623-2198.

6. RANCHO LA PUENTE
15415 E. DON JULIAN ROAD, CITY OF INDUSTRY

Two adobes stand here, the first built in 1842 by William Workman, co-founder of the first banking house in Los Angeles. In 1876, the bank's failure bankrupted Workman, who shot and killed himself in his office in this building. Workman's half of the original 48,470-acre Rancho La Puente (Ranch of the Bridge) was reduced to 75 acres because of his financial calamities. In 1920, Workman's grandson, Walter Temple, built a more modern adobe nearby. Today, the Homestead Museum offers free tours of both homes and the family cemetery. (818) 968-8492.

7. SANCHEZ ADOBE MUSEUM
946 N. ADOBE AVE., MONTEBELLO

Dona Casilda Soto de Lobo built the little place on the banks of the Rio Hondo in 1845 to fulfill a condition of ownership of the 2,363-acre Rancho la Merced. But the adobe house carries the name and legends of Juan Matias Sanchez, who took over the property seven years later. He lived rich and died poor, and in the end his family lost the house. Open to the public. (213) 887-4592.

8. RANCHO LOS ALAMITOS
6400 BIXBY HILL ROAD, LONG BEACH

Originally built in the early 1800s by retired soldier Juan Jose Nieto, it was renovated in 1842 by Abel Stearns as a home for his 15-year-old bride, Arcadia Bandini. Later the Bixby family bought the 26,000-acre Ranch of the Little Cottonwoods and lived here from 1881 to 1968. Open to the public. (310) 431-3541.

9. RANCHO LOS CERRITOS
4600 VIRGINIA ROAD, LONG BEACH

Jonathan Temple built this adobe and redwood house in 1843 on a bluff overlooking the Los Angeles River. Besides a museum, it houses a research library of California history. Open to the public. (310) 570-1755.

10. DOMINGUEZ ADOBE
18127 S. ALAMEDA ST., COMPTON

Nearly a dozen cities were carved out of Rancho San Pedro, the 76,000-acre grant given to Juan Jose Dominguez in 1784 by the Spanish crown. His grand-nephew, Don Manuel, inherited the ranch and began building the U-shaped, one-story adobe in 1825. Don Manuel and his bride, Maria Engracia Cota, lived here for 55 years and raised 10 children, six of whom survived to inherit more than 40,000 acres. Open to the public. (213) 636-6030.

11. VICENTE LUGO ADOBE
6360 E. GAGE AVE., BELL GARDENS

For nearly 200 years, this was the heart of the vast 29,413-acre Rancho San Antonio, and home of Don Antonio Maria Lugo, a Spanish cavalier, his heir, Don Vicente Lugo, and later Henry T. Gage, a former California governor who got the home as part of his wife's dowry. Restoration work should be completed and the adobe open to the public around March, 1997. (310) 927-7986.

12. GILMORE ADOBE
6301 W. 3RD ST., LOS ANGELES

Shrouded by vegetation in the middle of Farmers Market sits a 166-year-old adobe house. It was once the residence of Antonio Jose Rocha II in the middle of Rancho La Brea. In 1880, Arthur F. Gilmore bought the property. His son, Earl Gilmore, founded Farmers Market. In 1976, the A.F. Gilmore Co. turned the adobe into its private offices. Not open to the public.

■ Gilmore Field—"Home of the Hollywood Stars," see Page 71.

13. AVILA ADOBE
10 OLVERA ST., LOS ANGELES

Built in 1818 by Francisco Avila, once mayor of the city, this 176-year-old adobe—the oldest in the Los Angeles city limits—was occupied in the 1930s by the indomitable Christine Sterling, the "Mother of Olvera Street." Open to the public. (213) 625-5045.

NOT SHOWN ON MAP:

Sepulveda Adobe: In the oak-dotted hills, across Mulholland Highway from the main body of Malibu Creek State Park, is an arm of parkland called Liberty Canyon. Behind a chain-link fence sits the Sepulveda Adobe. (800) 533-PARK.

Adobe Flores: Built in the 1840s and reportedly the last headquarters of the Mexican army, this private residence is listed in the National Register of Historic Places and is a cultural landmark in South Pasadena. 500 block Garfield Avenue.

Casa de Adobe: This charming casa was a creation of the flamboyant Charles Lummis, founder of the Southwest Museum. 4605 N. Figueroa St., Los Angeles. (213) 221-2163.

CALL BEFORE VISITING:

Lopez Adobe, 1100 Pico St., San Fernando (818) 898-1200.
La Casa de la Centinela Adobe, 7634 Midfield Ave., Inglewood (310) 649-6272.
Pio Pico Mansion, Pio Pico State Historic Park, 6003 S. Pioneer Blvd., Whittier (310) 695-1217.
Casa Adobe de San Rafael, 1330 Dorothy Dr., Glendale (818) 548-2147.
Don Vicente de la Osa Adobe, 16756 Moorpark St., Encino (818) 784-4849.
La Casa Vieja de Lopez, 330 S. Santa Anita St., San Gabriel (818) 457-3035 or (818) 457-3040.
Leonis Adobe, 23537 Calabasas Road, Calabasas (818) 222-6511.
Andres Pico Adobe, 10940 Sepulveda Blvd., Mission Hills (818) 365-7810.
Tomas Sanchez Adobe, 3725 Don Felipe Dr., Los Angeles. Closed to the public.

The Dominguez Adobe in Compton, originally part of Rancho San Pedro.

Los Angeles Times

69

Andres Pico Adobe in Mission Hills.

Mitsu Yakusawa / Los Angeles Times

The Kathy Fiscus Vigil

In 1949 all of Los Angeles—as least as much of it as had television then—watched on small, primitive screens as efforts to save a little girl's life played out in stark black and white.

The 27 1/2-hour telecast (on KTLA Channel 5) is credited with originating live TV news, proving television's power to convey immediate emotions as it focused on the attempt to rescue 3-year-old Kathy Fiscus of San Marino, who had fallen into an abandoned well constructed of a pipe only 14 inches in diameter and more than 100 feet deep.

On April 9, Kathy had been playing in the tall, spring grass in an open field. Then, in an instant, she disappeared. Only her faint cries could be heard.

Kathy's mother, Alice, called for help and emergency crews soon converged.

For two days and nights, the effort to save her transfixed the city. Crowds gathered outside music and appliance store windows to watch on TV; others shared their sets with neighbors.

By the time TV crews arrived, firemen had already slipped air hoses down the 45-year-old shaft. Crowds of spectators, who had heard of the rescue on radio or seen it on TV, had to be held back by police.

Volunteers answered calls for people who could maneuver in the cramped shaft. Among them was a former coal miner who had sworn he would never go underground again, a former Navy diver and jockeys.

Alice Fiscus refused to give up hope. At one point Kathy had managed to hold on to a rope. She was pulled up a few feet, but her tiny hands lost their grip and she slid back down.

Tension grew at every setback, but the digging went on. A shaft was excavated parallel to the pipe, but when workers tried to descend, the sides crumbled. Another

Thousands of spectators gathered to watch as emergency crews and volunteers worked to free Kathy Fiscus from the shaft. Thousands more watched live TV coverage.

Los Angeles Times

shaft on the other side soon began to fill with water. Hourly reports let the public know how close rescuers were. Kathy had slid 94 feet down the shaft.

A microphone dangled into the pipe picked up what rescuers thought was Kathy's breathing. The digging resumed with renewed fervor.

For 50 hours, volunteers and city workers raced the clock as television cameras rolled. When they finally cut through the corroded pipe, Kathy was dead.

The family physician announced that she had probably died within two hours of slipping into the well. The coroner's report said that Kathy died from lack of oxygen because her knees were pressed against her chest.

Kathy Fiscus at age 3 in a family photo.

The dirty and tired rescue workers, along with a crowd of a hundreds or more, wept openly. So did thousands more listening to the radio or watching the new medium of television.

The Fiscus case was a turning point in TV history. Its marathon live reporting from the scene taught executives and audiences the potential of the news camera.

The old well that claimed the life of Kathy Fiscus has long since been filled in. There is no trace of it on what is now an athletic field at San Marino High School. The nearest reference is a bronze marker behind the San Marino City Library. Like the one on Kathy's grave, it recalls "a little girl who brought the world together—for a moment."

Home of the Hollywood Stars

When CBS broke ground for an 80,000-square-foot addition to its Television City complex in 1991, excavators unearthed the broken sections of an old baseball dugout.

The dugout once sheltered the triple-A Hollywood Stars in Gilmore Field, and was part of a sports complex that included Gilmore Stadium and the Pan Pacific Auditorium built on 287 unincorporated acres known as Gilmore Island.

Arthur Fremont Gilmore brought his family to Los Angeles from Illinois in

Gilmore Field and CBS studios in 1952, separated by Genessee Avenue. Gilmore birthplace is in trees above studios.

1874, started a dairy business and eventually made enough money to buy part of Rancho La Brea, roughly bounded by Beverly Boulevard, 3rd Street, Fairfax and La Brea avenues.

While drilling a water well in 1903, Gilmore struck oil. Before gas stations became common, Gilmore's son, Earl, used to take gasoline from the family refinery, load it in five-gallon cans and drive a buckboard down Wilshire Boulevard to sell it to an occasional motorist.

When Earl's father died in 1918, he owned 24 oil wells producing about 8,000 barrels a day. Earl founded the Gilmore Petroleum Co., later the Gilmore Oil Co., and went on to establish Red Lion gasoline stations up and down the West Coast.

In 1934 Gilmore built the Farmers Market at 3rd and Fairfax to help 18 Depression-era farmers sell their produce. Over the years, it has expanded to accommodate gift shops, more produce stalls and restaurants.

That same year, Gilmore put up $134,000 to build Gilmore Stadium at the southeast corner of Fairfax and Beverly. An aviation and sports enthusiast, he had planned to build the stadium for midget car racing, with grandstands on two sides. But Tom Lieb, head football coach at Loyola University, talked Gilmore into building stands on three sides and promised to have his team play there.

The old stadium also hosted other teams, including the Los Angeles Bulldogs and Hollywood Bears professional football teams, Los Angeles City College, Pepperdine University and some high schools. In 1936, the 18,500-seat stadium was overflowing with 19,300 fans who came to see the Detroit Lions play the Green Bay Packers.

Gilmore sold the stadium to CBS in 1950, and that year's Thanksgiving Night Grand Prix was the last race run on its track. Two years later, CBS built Television City on the site.

Gilmore Field was built in 1939, when the oil magnate paid $200,000 to put up the Stars' home park. An overflow crowd of 12,500 turned out on opening day to watch the Stars battle the Seattle Rainiers.

Bing Crosby, Jack Benny and Al Jolson were there. Rudy Vallee brought his 16-millimeter home-movie camera. And Dia Gable, recently divorced from Clark, sat behind home plate. George Burns and Gracie Allen had box seats along the third base line.

At the ballpark, bets were made just outside the gate, stands were about 15 feet from the base lines and no alcohol was sold. In 1958, the park was torn down with little fanfare.

More than 10 million sports fans saw events from baseball to broncobusting at Gilmore's two sports arenas. Thousands more saw attractions ranging from the Harlem Globetrotters to Elvis Presley at the Pan Pacific, which burned in 1989 and has been razed.

All that remains of the Gilmores' 287-acre island now is 31 acres at 3rd and Fairfax, where a 19th-century adobe building sits. It is the birthplace of Earl Gilmore and the headquarters of the A.F. Gilmore Co., which manages the Farmers Market.

Labor Landmarks

Southland sites that call to mind the labor movement's long struggle for better wages and working conditions.

----

1. SAMUEL GOMPERS MIDDLE SCHOOL
234 E. 112TH ST., LOS ANGELES

Near the turn of the century, the nationwide rallying cry of the fledgling labor movement led by Samuel Gompers, the father of the American Federation of Labor (now the AFL-CIO), was the eight-hour day. The call helped attract workers to the cause of unionism. California instituted the eight-hour day for women workers in 1913; it later was extended to minors. In 1974, adult men were finally brought under the state wage and hour law. Gompers always summed up what he wanted for his union members as "more."

For more than a year after the Samuel Gompers Middle School was named after the union leader in 1936, PTA members protested. They wanted it named in honor of humorist Will Rogers. In the early 1950s, the Lakewood Unified School District also named one of its elementary schools after the union leader.

UFW official David Martinez, with Mayor Richard Riordan and Councilwoman Gloria Molina, holds sign as street is renamed for Cesar Chavez.

Rick Corrales / Los Angeles Times

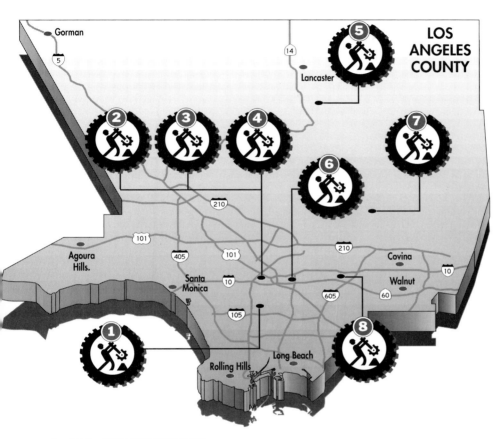

2. 3RD STREET TUNNEL
HILL AND 3RD STREETS, LOS ANGELES

On Jan. 20, 1900, 12 workmen were buried alive and others were disabled by a landslide in the half-completed 3rd Street Tunnel. Two days earlier, two workmen had been killed in a cave-in at the same site. The contractors declared they had no liability for workers injured on the job, and city officials decided that since it was an accident, no liability could be attached. Angry Los Angeles trade unionists lobbied year after year following the accidents to get worker's compensation legislation to protect workers like these. It took more than a decade, but in 1911, legislators enacted a voluntary plan of compensation benefits. Two years later, benefits were made compulsory, regardless of fault.

3. EMBASSY HOTEL AND AUDITORIUM
851 S. GRAND AVE., LOS ANGELES

Originally built as a concert hall in 1914, the auditorium served as a rallying

Still standing today are the ruins of Llano's combination hotel, dining room and meeting hall. Most of the original residents left for Louisiana in 1917.

J. Albert Diaz / Los Angeles Times

place for progressive organizations and immigrant unions from the 1920s to the 1950s. In 1933, Rose Pesotta, a Jewish woman who would later become vice president of the International Ladies' Garment Workers Union, led 1,500 dressmakers in an organizing meeting here, launching a month-long strike which won them a small wage increase and recognition. The hotel/auditorium was closed after the earthquake of Jan. 17, 1994.

4. LOS ANGELES TIMES
1ST STREET AND BROADWAY, LOS ANGELES

Early on the morning of Oct. 1, 1910, a huge explosion tore apart the Los Angeles Times building on the northeast corner of 1st Street and Broadway, setting off a roaring fire that killed 20 men. The anti-union paper immediately blamed the bomb blast on leaders of organized labor. The confession of two ironworkers' leaders, John and Jim McNamara, discredited labor's fight against the open shop, and organized labor suffered a severe setback as a result of the bombing. The bitter and often violent struggle between labor and capitalists would grip the nation until the outbreak of World War II. However, Los Angeles, which embraced the open shop principle, remained mostly on the sidelines.

The Times building was rebuilt on the same site, with a plaque commemorating the men who died. When that building was torn down in 1938, the plaque went into storage. Today, the site, later occupied by a state building that was also torn down, is fenced off and filled with six-foot-high weeds. Plans for a new civic center office tower on the site have been collecting dust since 1987.

5. LLANO
ON HWY 128, WEST OF LLANO P.O., NEAR BIG ROCK CREEK

Crumbling chimneys and walls are lingering monuments to almost a thousand people who once labored in this water-scarce community, officially known as the Llano del Rio Cooperative Colony. Located in the Antelope Valley not far from the site of present-day Llano, the first settlement was established in about 1888, possibly by Quakers. The peak year was 1895, when 100 people lived in or near the community. By 1900 drought and the failure of an irrigation project had dried up the first Llano.

In 1914 the town was resettled by Los Angeles Socialists under the guidance of attorney and former mayoral candidate Job Harriman, who wanted to prove the theory of cooperative living. Between 1915 and 1917, Llano was the largest town in the Antelope Valley and at its high point had a population of about 1,000.

But within a year, the cooperative had failed—due to lack of cooperation, some said. Fourteen people would be assigned a job, but only four would do the work. A second problem was the recurring water shortage. Most of the townsfolk left for the timbered country of Louisiana, where Harriman purchased 20,000 acres to start another colony that he named Newllano. The Llano they left behind eventually went bankrupt, even though a few hardy souls remained. Today, Llano has a population of about 350 with a golf course, post office, gas station and grocery store.

6. CESAR CHAVEZ AVENUE
THROUGH BOYLE HEIGHTS AND EAST LOS ANGELES

A former apricot picker and founder of the United Farm Workers union, Cesar Chavez fought to organize farm workers in California's Central Valley and fasted to bring attention to the plight of the workers and their families. In 1965, Chavez began urging consumers to boycott table grapes, eventually forcing the growers to the bargaining table. Ten years later, the state legislature passed the Agriculture Labor Relations Act, the landmark law that gave farm workers the right to collective bargaining and to seek redress for unfair job practices.

In honor of the late labor leader, the Los Angeles County Board of Supervisors and City Council renamed Brooklyn Avenue, one of the city's oldest streets, which extends from the Los Angeles River to Atlantic Boulevard.

7. UPTON SINCLAIR'S HOUSE
464 N. MYRTLE AVE., MONROVIA

Pulitzer Prize-winning author and social reformer Upton Sinclair shocked the nation in 1906 when he described the filth in Chicago's slaughterhouses and the horrors of working conditions there in his book "The Jungle." Government inspection of meat began soon after his book was published, but it wasn't until 1970 that the Occupational Safety and Health Act was passed.

After Pasadena became too crowded for him, Sinclair moved to Monrovia, where he lived from 1942 to 1966.

8. STRAWBERRY FIELDS
BOUNDED BY RUSH STREET, CENTRAL AVENUE, WHITTIER NARROWS RECREATION CENTER AND THE RIO HONDO RIVER, SOUTH EL MONTE

In May, 1933, years before developers paved over the strawberry fields that were part of the city of El Monte, several thousand pickers went on strike, protesting their low wages of 9 cents an hour. Their leader was Zenaida (Sadie) Castro, a feisty Mexican American and one of the few pickers who spoke English. When she wasn't holding off the union busters, she was cooking rice and beans for the strikers. As news of the strike spread, Mexican and Japanese immigrant workers in the celery and onion fields of Venice, Culver City and Santa Monica demanded higher wages. Within a few months, pickers' wages were increased to 20 cents an hour.

■ **"Heyday and Decline of a Lively Barrio," see below.**

The Heyday and Decline of a Lively Barrio

For almost a century, El Monte basked in the bucolic prosperity created by thriving walnut groves, strawberry fields and dairy farms. It was renowned as "The Garden of Los Angeles County."

But gardens need tending. By 1915 a few desperate Mexican families, fleeing revolutionary turmoil and poverty, began to trickle north, looking for job opportunities in the lush oasis of the San Gabriel Valley. They set up tents on a tree-shaded, 56-acre site that stretched along the Rio Hondo River, bound by what are now Valley Boulevard, Lower Azusa Road and Arden Drive.

They named their camp after its German owner, Robert Hicks, and his son Stanley, who for the next three decades would profit by recruiting contract crews of Mexican farm laborers from the camp.

By the 1920s, the trickle of immigrants had become a flood, spilling over into four nearby barrios: Wiggins, Flores, Granada and Hayes camps.

In many ways, life at Hicks Camp replicated what residents had left behind in Mexico. The small houses, built without foundations out of used lumber salvaged from old boxcars, had dirt floors. Paths worn through crabgrass created the dirt roads. There were no street lights or sewers. While the able-bodied toiled in nearby fields, old men slept in the sun and old women tended vegetable gardens. Residents swam and picnicked at the nearby river. There were regular dances behind San Juan Bosco, the camp's Roman Catholic church.

Father John V. Coffield walks with two of his young parishioners in 1951.

Los Angeles Times

During the Depression, the U.S. government undertook the forced repatriation of thousands of Mexican immigrants. But the people of Hicks Camp refused to be cowed. They went on strike, protesting the 9-cent-an-hour wage they were paid for their labor in the surrounding fields.

When the anti-Latino "Zoot Suit Riots" broke out in Los Angeles in 1943, local toughs also threatened Hicks Camp. The barrio's children hid in trees, clenching rocks, ready to throw. But law enforcement officers clad in riot gear responded by heading off the would-be attackers.

At the time, the El Monte barrios' sons were serving in the U.S. armed forces. But after World War II, many of those veterans and their families were evicted from nearby Wiggins Camp, south of the railroad tracks, to make way for industrial expansion. Prohibited from moving into more affluent Anglo parts of town, some found shelter with families from Hicks.

Their landlord charged $9.50 a month for rent, which included leveling the dirt streets after heavy rains, but not trash pickup. More than 600 tenants were forced to dump garbage near the riverbed, inviting rats to infest the camp. Periodically, water pipes—which had been installed some years before—broke and cesspools overflowed, causing outbreaks of contagious diseases.

In the late 1940s, led by San Juan Bosco's Spanish-speaking pastor, Father John V. Coffield, the residents decided their community needed a few improvements, including a name change to Hicksville. A civic committee composed of seven elected officers and three advisers set out to strengthen the community ties with the city and improve living conditions. The priest, affectionately known by many as Juanote (Big John), helped the barrio residents raise funds to buy the land their homes sat on. But the $40,000 price tag ultimately proved too high.

So, at Coffield's urging, Hicksville residents demanded that the Los Angeles County Board of Supervisors give them better schools, housing, parks and garbage collection.

In 1954, some camp residents welcomed Hollywood's selection of Hicksville—with its miserable, dilapidated homes and weed-choked yards—to portray a poor, backward Southern town in the all-black musical "Carmen Jones."

As signs of drugs and gang activity increased at Hicksville, talk of "redevelopment" began. Finally, in 1973, 57 tiny ramshackle wood-frame homes were leveled, forcing the final exodus of about 200 close-knit Hicksville residents.

Black History in L.A.

Historic sites honor the many roles played by
African-Americans in Los Angeles' development.

1. VAL VERDE
SANTA CLARITA VALLEY, ROUGHLY BOUNDED BY
INTERSTATE 5, CALIFORNIA 126 AND HASLEY CANYON
AND SAN MARTINEZ ROADS

The community began in the mid-1920s as kind of a black Palm Springs. Entertainers such as Count Basie, Duke Ellington, Della Reese and Billy Eckstein visited the rural summer retreat and occasionally gave impromptu concerts at the Val Verde Park. It lost some of its luster in the late 1960s when other, once-segregated vacation spots dropped their color barriers. Eventually, farm workers moved into the cabins.

2. BUNCHE HALL
UCLA, 405 HILGARD AVE., LOS ANGELES

Ralph J. Bunche was the first black American to win a Nobel Prize, capturing the Peace Prize for his efforts to end a Middle East war in 1950. He attended John Adams Junior High School, Jefferson High School and UCLA before earning his doctorate at Harvard and beginning his career as a diplomat. The building named for him is on the northeast side of the campus.

3. SAKS FIFTH AVENUE
9600 WILSHIRE BLVD., BEVERLY HILLS

Local black architect Paul R. Williams designed the Art Moderne-style store in 1937 and the Los Angeles County Courthouse at 1st and Hill streets in 1958. Williams, who died in 1980, also designed the Tudor mansion in Pasadena used in the "Batman" TV series, the Second Baptist Church in South-Central Los Angeles and homes for several stars, including Frank Sinatra, Cary Grant and Lon Chaney Sr. Williams became the first black member of the American Institute of Architects.

4. MUSEUM IN BLACK
4331 DEGNAN BLVD., LOS ANGELES.

On a quiet block between 43rd Street and 43rd Place in Leimert Park, museum owner Brian Breye has a dazzling array of African masks and black memorabilia.

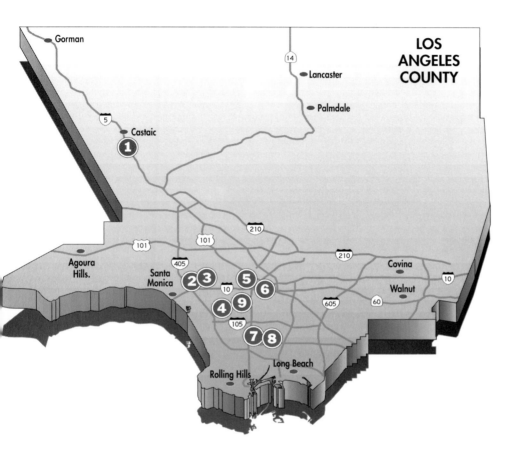

Map of Los Angeles County showing locations: Gorman, Lancaster, Palmdale, Castaic, Agoura Hills, Santa Monica, Covina, Walnut, Long Beach, Rolling Hills.

5. THE OAK TREE
1100 BLOCK, SOUTH HOBART STREET, LOS ANGELES

Cornelius Johnson, a black athlete who won gold medals in the 1936 Olympics in Berlin, was snubbed by Adolf Hitler when the Nazi leader refused to shake hands with blacks. The Olympic Committee presented team members with three-inch sapling oak trees. Today, Johnson's oak has grown to 40 feet and is visible from the street.

6. BIDDY MASON PARK
333 S. SPRING ST., LOS ANGELES

A former slave, nurse and midwife, Biddy Mason purchased this land for $250 more than a century ago and opened a refuge for black families. A striking 8-by-81-foot mural in the tree-shaded mini-park and rest area memorializes Mason's long and humanitarian life.

Los Angeles Times

Descendants of Biddy Mason look at a mural on South Spring Street that details the life of the former slave, nurse and midwife.

7. FIRE STATION NO. 30
1401 S. CENTRAL AVE., LOS ANGELES

Opened as a segregated facility in 1924, this dilapidated, scarred old building has sat vacant since its closure in 1980. It is the city's oldest fire station that was completely staffed by African-Americans.

8. CALIFORNIA EAGLE
4071-4075 S. CENTRAL AVE., LOS ANGELES

From 1879 to 1964, the California Eagle, dedicated to improving the lives of African-Americans, was the longest-publishing black newspaper on the West Coast. It began as the Advocate, and its masthead read: "Devoted to the cause of good government and the advance of the Afro-American." The newspaper led the fight to gain black support for women's suffrage in California in 1911. Later, the paper was renamed the California Eagle, and journalist and labor activist Charlotta Bass became editor. Today, S & J Appliances occupies the site.
■ More about California Eagle, see Page 83

9. HOLMES AVENUE SCHOOL
5108 HOLMES AVE., LOS ANGELES

The small, one-story, wood-frame 51st Street School, built in 1910, became the first all-black school in Los Angeles. Bessie Bruington Burke became the school's first black teacher and principal. When the school burned down in 1922, it was rebuilt and renamed the Holmes Avenue School.
■ "Honoring L.A.'s Black Founders," see Page 85.

Arnet Hartsfield Collection

Pioneering African-American Journalist

For more than 50 years, Charlotta Spears Bass defended and taught and shaped Los Angeles' growing black community.

The pioneering African-American journalist, who became a labor activist and the Progressive Party's candidate for vice president of the United States, arrived in Los Angeles in 1910, destined to become the editor of the California Eagle, the West Coast's oldest black newspaper.

At 36 she came to Los Angeles from Rhode Island. She found a job as a paper-girl, collecting and selling subscriptions to a small black newspaper named the Advocate, which had been founded by John J. Neimore in 1879.

Charlotta Spears was soon promoted to helping Neimore in the office for $5 a week. And within two years of arriving in Los Angeles, she found herself at the helm of the newspaper.

Neimore died in 1912. The newspaper went on the auction block as Spears stood by, too poor to bid. A neighbor, a second-hand store dealer, saw her anxiety. "If I buy it for you, do you think you can earn enough to (re)pay me?" he asked.

Spears said yes. The neighbor bought it with a $50 bid and handed over the deed. With assets of printing presses and $10, Spears began her long career with vision, courage and perseverance—and $150 in overdue bills.

The same year, Spears changed the paper's name and her own. The Advocate became the California Eagle, and she married Joseph B. Bass, a founder of the

Fire Station No. 30 opened in 1924. A year later, 30 of the original 32 black firefighters posed with engines outside the now-closed firehouse.

Charlotta Bass, editor of the California Eagle, the West Coast's oldest black newspaper.

Topeka Plaindealer, who had been caught up in the urge to "go West."

This new team began a fearless campaign against segregation and discrimination in Los Angeles.

In 1914, Bass tried but failed to halt the making of D.W. Griffith's film "The Birth of a Nation," which glorifies the Ku Klux Klan. But she forced Griffith to cut some offensive scenes.

As World War I was raging two years later, Bass launched her own fight—this time for fairer voting rights.

In the November, 1916, election, she noticed a tab on the right-hand corner of each ballot with instructions that said, "Tear off if the voter is a Negro." Black Election Board members refused, and no such tabs appeared again on Los Angeles ballots.

Racism showed itself on many fronts, and in 1925, after the Eagle printed a letter exposing KKK plans to take over Watts, the Knights of the White Camellia sued the paper for libel.

More than two months later, on June 25, in a crowded courtroom, the California Eagle, circulation about 12,000, beat the Klan and the libel charge. Soon, Bass began getting anonymous, insulting phone calls. And late one evening, eight white-hooded men showed up at her office. They cut their visit short when she pulled a gun out of a desk drawer and aimed it at them.

By 1938, the Eagle was extending its reach, taking its message to the airwaves. Its columns about sports, drama and opinion were heard six nights a week on station KGFJ.

On the eve of World War II, Bass and the Eagle began a campaign against restrictive housing covenants, part of the common "Jim Crow laws," and supported black families trying to move into all-white areas. Among them were Henry and Texanna Laws, who in 1936 had bought a house on 92nd Street in Watts, then a mostly white and Latino community.

However, the law said they could own it but not live in it. They took the matter to court. After eight years, the case reached the California Supreme Court, which upheld the Lawses' and the California Eagle's position. Restrictive real estate covenants became unconstitutional.

Bass was in her 60s one winter day in 1941 when she heard a report of bonfires and mock lynchings at Fremont High School. She went there to cover the incident and found herself counseling the angry students.

"Negroes just can't go to school with white people any more. They can't mix," one student told her.

"Oh, I don't know," answered the woman who was walking picket lines to protest segregation in the aircraft industry. "I just can't make myself believe that you would object to my child going to this school or even living next door to you. I believe we would learn to like each other if we ever really became acquainted."

When police tried to stop their discussion, a white student protested, "We like this woman; she is giving us good advice." But police ordered the group to disperse.

By 1951, Bass had sold the Eagle to pursue new challenges.

She had already served as the first African-American on the Los Angeles County grand jury, and she lost her first political campaign, a City Council race, in 1945.

For 40 years, Bass had supported the Republican Party in her newspaper, but after World War II, her thinking changed, and she joined the new Progressive Party. She lost to future Los Angeles Mayor Sam Yorty in her bid for a congressional seat in 1950, the same year she was labeled a Communist for traveling to a peace conference in Czechoslovakia.

She made her last run at politics at 78 as the Progressive candidate for vice president—the first black woman candidate for the office—on the ticket with presidential candidate Vincent Hallinan.

The Eagle folded in 1964, a year after the man who bought it from Bass became a judge. The Eagle's last home, on Central Avenue, is now an appliance store.

And the woman who made the paper's reputation died in 1969. She was 95.

Honoring L.A.'s Black Founders

In the 1950s, a plaque was installed in El Pueblo de Los Angeles State Historic Park, paying tribute to 11 families who founded Los Angeles on Sept. 4, 1781, after a long trek from Mexico. They were called pobladores, and more than half of them were black. Those early Angelenos of African descent had Spanish surnames, and their ethnicity would not have been known had the plaque not indicated it.

The plaque soon vanished without a trace.

Rumor had it that several Recreation and Parks commissioners had been displeased by the public display of the role blacks played in the city's founding.

That plaque was replaced in 1981—marking the city's bicentennial—with a simple bronze tablet that tells the pobladores' names, race, sex and age. It was installed through the trailblazing efforts of Miriam Matthews, California's first college-trained black librarian.

There are no grandiose monuments, streets or landmarks named for the 44 pobladores. And although it may not be possible to trace their presence in concrete and stone, their memories can be followed from place to place across the city's two centuries of history.

Bessie Bruington Burke and pupils at 51st Street School, where she was L.A.'s first black teacher and principal.

Courtesy of Holmes Elementary School

All the original settlers, including black pobladores Luis Quintero and Antonio Mesa, married racially mixed women and built their makeshift houses of willow branches, tule reeds and mud. After several floods, however, they relocated the little pueblo in 1815 to a site just north of the Old Plaza Church. Three years later, the plaza was moved to its present location near Alameda and Macy streets.

At the turn of the century, the African-American community had grown to more than 2,200 people, spreading from 1st and Los Angeles streets to Boyle Heights. West of downtown, many blacks settled along Jefferson Boulevard, between Normandie and Western avenues and in an area bounded by Beverly Boulevard and Rampart, Temple and Hyans streets. Others bought parcels of land about five miles south of downtown from an Irish farmer named James Furlong.

In 1905, Furlong subdivided his land bounded by Long Beach Avenue and Alameda, 50th and 55th streets. He sold his lots to black families for the going price of $750.

From the start, the Furlong Tract was a working-class area, settled by people like the Guillebeaus, Postells and Hickses who were barred from other areas by restrictive racial covenants or high prices. The area had convenient transportation (the Main Street car lines ran through the center of the neighborhood). Many families worked for what was then the generous sum of $3.75 a day at such nearby plants as the Cottonseed Oil Mill, the Hercules Foundry and Pioneer Paper Co.

Some families lived in tents while they built their modest homes. Eventually, the tract had more than 200 houses, grocery stores, a pharmacy, doctors' offices, a florist, dry cleaners, an ice cream parlor, a real estate office, an icehouse, a community hall, three churches and a school.

Built in 1910, the one-story, wood-frame 51st Street School became the first all-black school in Los Angeles. It hired white teachers because discriminatory hiring kept black teachers out of many cities in the state, including Los Angeles.

The year after it was built, Bessie Bruington Burke became the school's first black teacher and eight years later the school's first black principal.

"Mrs. Burke used to make us toe the line, and it wasn't hard since most of the youngsters were afraid of her," recalled Paul Postell, who attended the school. "She was one of those principals who didn't have to say much. She would just look at you."

The school burned down in 1922, and it was renamed the Holmes Avenue School when it was rebuilt.

In 1933, the Long Beach earthquake damaged some of the Furlong Tract homes. A few families started moving to other neighborhoods, and the tract began to decline.

The once neat single-family homes, many with vegetable gardens, were torn down in the 1940s to build Pueblo del Rio, a low-income housing project. The residents scattered and all that remains are a school and the memories of those who grew up there.

WPA Projects

Artistic and architectural treasures created during the Depression by the Works Projects Administration.

----

1. POLYTECHNIC HIGH SCHOOL
1600 ATLANTIC AVE., LONG BEACH

Long Beach has a rich heritage of WPA art projects, largely because many of the city's public buildings were seriously damaged in a 1933 earthquake and were rebuilt during the years when the WPA was at its height. The government ordered that its 14 public art projects reflect themes from the Long Beach community. Ten of those remain, including a mural in muted browns and blues in the stairwell at Poly High School. By Jean Swiggett and Ivan Bartlett, it depicts dockworkers unloading crates of fruit, sailors standing with folded arms, surfers at the beach and women working in a fish cannery.

The William D. Davies Memorial Building in Altadena.

Al Seib / Los Angeles Times

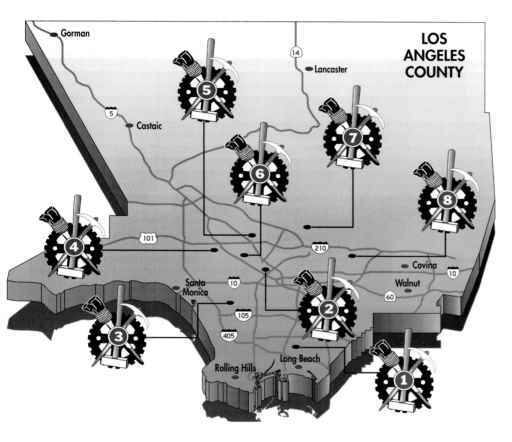

2. U.S. NAVAL AND MARINE RESERVE TRAINING CENTER
1700 STADIUM WAY, LOS ANGELES

This historic site in Chavez Ravine was once known as the "pesthouse" because smallpox victims were confined there until the 1920s. It was rebuilt in Deco-Moderne style typical of public buildings of the 1930s: streamlined, smooth surfaces; spare and abstract ornamentation, and monument-like stone steps leading to an imposing white portico supported by huge stone pillars.

■ **This is where the march toward Latino freedom began, see Page 92.**

3. MOSAIC WALL
CENTINELA PARK, REDONDO BOULEVARD AND FLORENCE AVENUE IN INGLEWOOD

A mosaic wall eight feet high and 240 feet long stands at the back entrance to Centinela Park. The 53-year-old work by WPA artist Helen Lundeberg depicts the development of transportation, from oxcarts to streetcars to trains and airplanes.

The 1940 dedication of statue of kneeling harpist atop the Hollywood Bowl fountain.

Los Angeles Times

4. HOLLYWOOD BOWL FOUNTAIN
2301 N. HIGHLAND AVE., HOLLYWOOD

A concrete figure of a kneeling woman playing a harp atop an Art Deco-inspired fountain greets motorists negotiating Cahuenga Pass in front of the Hollywood Bowl. Down the street are more examples of Art Deco and Moderne styles, blended into the WPA-built science and liberal arts buildings of Hollywood High School, 1521 N. Highland Ave.

5. BURBANK POST OFFICE
135 E. OLIVE AVE., BURBANK

The Los Angeles area has the nation's second-largest concentration of WPA art, after New York City. This postal branch is graced by a two-panel mural saluting the city's most famous industries—filmmaking and aeronautics. Titled "People of Burbank," the 1940 work by Barse Miller fits in with the building's tile and wrought-iron Spanish mission motif.

6. GRIFFITH PARK CLUBHOUSE
GRIFFITH DRIVE, LOS ANGELES

On Oct. 3, 1933, tragedy struck in the Mineral Wells area of Griffith Park. More

Mural celebrating aeronautics industry in the Burbank Post Office.

Joel P. Lugavere / Los Angeles Times

than 1,500 public-relief workers in the park came rushing to put out a brush fire. Some climbed down into the steep canyon to fight the blaze, but having no fire-fighting experience, 29 of the workers were engulfed by flames and died. Two years later the WPA rebuilt the clubhouse that had burned in the fire.

■ **Col. Griffith: both beast and benefactor, see Page 94.**

7. WILLIAM D. DAVIES MEMORIAL BUILDING
568 E. MT. CURVE AVE., ALTADENA

The heavy stones that form the building's base and massive fireplaces were hauled from the nearby arroyo by mule teams and unemployed Altadenans in the 1930s to construct this community building and auditorium. The building, which was untouched by the 1993 fire, was named for a member of the Theater Americana who lobbied for its construction. For almost 60 years, the nonprofit theatrical group has offered this place for playwrights to have their works produced.

8. ARCADIA PARK AND GOLF COURSE
405 S. SANTA ANITA AVE., ARCADIA

During World War I, this site was known as Ross Field, a U.S. balloon training school for more than 3,500 military personnel. WPA workers transformed the area into a park and golf course. Before opening day Oct. 12, 1938, the WPA crew christened each golf hole: The fifth is "Railroad" because it paralleled the Pacific Electric tracks; the 11th is "Wind" because the prevailing wind blows in players' faces, and the 16th is "Clubhouse Turn" because it was the first turn on pioneer Lucky Baldwin's original racetrack site. A plaque paying tribute to the WPA has been placed in storage because park personnel say they cannot find the right place to display it.

The scene on Broadway in Los Angeles in June, 1943, as a mob dragged zoot-suited passengers from a trolley.

Los Angeles Times

Where Latino March Toward Justice Began

In 1942, Sleepy Lagoon was a swimming hole for young Mexican Americans who weren't allowed to swim at segregated public pools. At night, it served as a lovers' paradise.

On Aug. 1, a party attended by Latino youths was held at a ranch house there. Gate crashers—alleged members of the 38th Street Gang—arrived and fighting quickly broke out. Some cars were overturned and windows smashed. After the melee, 21-year-old Jose Diaz was found beaten to death.

Within days, police had rounded up 600 youths for questioning; 24 of them were indicted for murder, setting the stage for the largest mass criminal trial in American history.

Two of the alleged gang members hired their own attorneys and were released. During the course of the investigation and trial, the other 22 suspects were held incommunicado; two were badly beaten by their police interrogators. All were denied clean clothing, showers and haircuts until late in the trial.

A Los Angeles sheriff's "expert" testified that people of Mexican descent were biologically predisposed to "a desire to kill or at least draw blood."

At trial, none of the witnesses ever testified that they saw anyone strike the victim. Some of the defendants couldn't even be placed at the scene.

The U.S. Office of War Information feared the campaign against the "boy gangs" might be a ploy by the Nazis attempting to cause civil unrest in America. Many of the inflammatory stories came from enemy wartime radio broadcasters such as Tokyo Rose and Axis Sally, reporting, "10,000 Mexicans were rounded up and put in concentration camps in Southern California."

In January, 1943, after a three-month trial, 12 defendants were convicted of murder. The jury acquitted five others and found the remaining five guilty of assault, but they were released because of time already spent in jail.

Portion of crowd in Hall of Justice greeting youths freed in Sleepy Lagoon slaying case.

Los Angeles Times

Charging that the young men were railroaded on racist grounds, concerned citizens organized to fight for their release. Eighteen months later, an appeals court overturned all the convictions. The appellate justices severely reprimanded Judge Charles W. Fricke for displaying prejudice and hostility toward the defendants. The court also criticized the prosecutors, who had improperly pointed out the clothing and haircuts of the defendants as evidence of their guilt.

But by then, the campaign against Latino young people—who were stereotyped as zoot-suited pachucos—had moved to the streets. (A typical "zoot suit" was an oversized, wide-shouldered jacket, baggy pants with eccentric suspenders and a wide-brimmed hat.)

A group of sailors reported they had been beaten by Latinos on Los Angeles' Main Street, and more than 200 other sailors, stationed at the Naval Armory in Chavez Ravine, went looking for revenge.

Over a two-week period, in May and June, 1943, police stood by while several thousand servicemen and civilians wandered the streets, drawing cheers from bystanders as they beat up Latino youths, stripping them of their draped jackets and pegged pants. The "zoot suit hoodlums" were blamed for staying at home and not going off to war. Yet some who wore the unconventional zoot suit actually were GIs on leave.

The Los Angeles City Council, refusing to take responsibility for what happened, responded to the situation by banning the victims' zoot suits within the city.

The Sleepy Lagoon slaying was never solved, but its impact extended far beyond the courtroom.

Today, the site of Sleepy Lagoon is a gritty industrial zone, but it is remembered as the symbolic starting point in Latinos' long march toward equal justice and opportunity in the Southwest.

Col. Griffith: Beast and Benefactor

The name of Col. Griffith Jenkins Griffith is one of the most recognizable in modern Los Angeles—Griffith Park, Griffith Observatory, Griffith Park Drive and Griffith Park Boulevard.

But in his time, the Welsh-born immigrant who made a fortune in mining—a man with luxurious tastes, civic generosity, an unquenchable thirst for alcohol and an

Col. Griffith Jenkins Griffith.

Security Pacific Collection

intemperate disposition—was best known not for his good deeds but his criminal ones, like shooting his wife in a drunken tirade.

In 1882, the colonel—his title courtesy of his buddies in the California National Guard—bought 4,071 acres of Rancho Los Feliz for $50,000.

In 1896, Griffith presented the city with a Christmas gift of the 3,015 acres of hills, green valleys, streams and meadows that today is Griffith Park, the biggest U.S. municipal park to be entirely surrounded by a city.

Griffith's wife, Mary Agnes Christina Mesmer, was a descendant of the Verdugo family, who received the King of Spain's first land grant in the region—the 36,000-acre Rancho San Rafael—which made her a landowner, too. The colonel asked her to deed him a piece of her land as collateral in a business deal. Being an obedient wife, she did. But later, when she asked for it back, Griffith blew his top.

His reputation as a man of temper was cemented by what happened then, on his vacation in 1903, at the Arcadia Hotel, an elaborate four-story seaside resort overlooking Santa Monica Bay.

On a late summer afternoon, the Griffiths took a leisurely walk on the beach. Mrs. Griffith returned to their room, and a short time later Griffith appeared with bloodshot

Los Angeles Times

Family strolls through wooded section of Griffith Park early in the century.

eyes, handed his wife her prayer book, ordered her to kneel and took out his pistol.

The Protestant Griffith accused his wife of being "in league with the Pope and the church to poison him so she could turn all his money over to the Catholics," according to the Griffith Park Quarterly. He told her to close her eyes and swear she had been a faithful wife. She said, "Darling, you know I have." Their 12-year-old son, she sobbed, needed his mother.

Griffith, very drunk, was unmoved by her claim of faithfulness and her plea of motherhood.

As Mrs. Griffith opened her eyes and saw the pistol barrel only inches away, she jerked her head, and the bullet went through her left eye.

Screaming in terror, she jumped through the open window and tumbled two stories to the roof of the veranda below, breaking an arm when she landed.

She dragged herself into a room. Screaming for help, she found a towel to hold over the eye, which was gushing blood.

The hotel manager answered her call for help and summoned the sheriff.

Griffith's attorney, the legendary Earl Rogers, came up with what was then a novel defense: trying to "prove that Mrs. Griffith had too much religion, and the colonel too much champagne," wrote a Los Angeles Times reporter. Rogers argued that Griffith was a victim of "alcohol insanity." The colonel was convicted of attempted murder, drew only a two-year sentence and left San Quentin a year later as a new man—sane, sober and still very rich.

He soon made further gifts, willing even more land and a substantial trust fund for the upkeep of the park, and for building an observatory and theater.

Despite the bloody shooting that cost her the sight in one eye—and because her religion forbade divorce—Mrs. Griffith stayed with her husband in their 17-room mansion until he died in 1919, at age 67. The mansion still stands on North Vermont Avenue, near the Roosevelt Golf Course.

Buried Treasure

Legends persist of buried gold, cash and jewels, even though treasure hunters keep digging and not finding.

----

1. CAMP 19
22550 EAST FORK ROAD, AZUSA

In 1853, near what would become Claremont, four outlaws robbed a stage carrying a Wells Fargo chest filled with $30,000. They fled up San Antonio Canyon, with a posse not far behind. The leader headed down the east fork of the San Gabriel River. Before he was shot down, he is said to have buried his money-laden saddlebags in a grove of oak trees, now believed to be part of State Prison Camp 19. The money was never recovered.

2. MONTEREY PARK
WEST OF GARFIELD AVENUE BETWEEN EL REPETTO DRIVE AND CORAL VIEW STREET

On April 14, 1874, Tiburcio Vasquez, a legendary Mexican bandido, and his gang of outlaws tortured and beat Alessandro Repetto, a prosperous Italian immigrant who owned a 5,000-acre ranch. Vasquez sent Repetto's nephew to a bank to withdraw the rancher's money, but suspicious bank officials called the sheriff, and the shaken boy told of the holdup. Meanwhile, Vasquez beat Repetto until he revealed two bags containing $40,000 in gold and silver.

Fleeing with the heavy loot as the sheriff arrived, the outlaws were seen burying something on Repetto's ranch. Repetto supposedly searched for his money for years in vain. Today, most of the ranch has been paved over.

Vasquez, who was hanged in 1875, left legends of buried treasure across Southern California.

3. SAN PEDRO HARBOR
On April 27, 1863, a small steam tug, the Ada Hancock, was dropping passengers off at San Pedro. Suddenly the tug lurched, and cold water flooded into the engine room. The boiler exploded, sinking the vessel. Twenty-six of the 53 passengers were lost, including William Ritchie, a Wells Fargo messenger carrying $10,000 in gold, and Fred E. Kerlin, who had $30,000 in cash strapped to his body. The money has never been found.

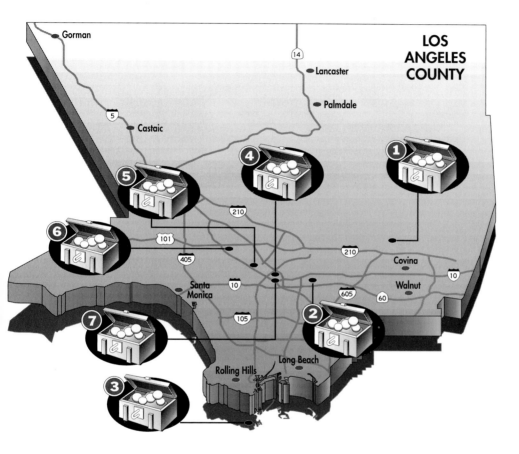

Gorman
14
Lancaster
Palmdale
5
Castaic
4
5
6
101
210
405
Santa Monica
10
105
210
Covina
Walnut
10
605
60
2
7
Rolling Hills
Long Beach
3

LOS ANGELES COUNTY

4. ELYSIAN PARK

835 ACADEMY ROAD, LOS ANGELES

Elysian (the ancient Greek word for "paradise") Park is, if you believe the tales, a 585-acre landscaped vault crammed with valuables buried more than 160 years ago by frightened residents. Many tales have been told of locals stashing gold coins and jewels in the hills, hoping to keep invading American troops from seizing them as Mexicans and Americans fought over Southern California. Francisco Avila, the mayor of the pueblo, built the first house on Olvera Street and became rich selling sheep and cattle. With no banks then in town, rumor holds, he placed his gold in tin cans, sealed and buried them under a pepper tree in what is now Elysian Park. When Avila died in 1831, the secret of his supposedly buried gold died with him.

San Pedro Harbor as it looked about the time the Ada Hancock sank with $10,000 in gold.

5. AMERICAN FILM INSTITUTE
2021 N. WESTERN AVE., HOLLYWOOD

Before the Sisters of Immaculate Heart of Mary bought the grounds in the early 1900s to establish a school, the famous Southland bandit Joaquin Murrieta is said to have buried his treasures on a hill here. Treasure seekers—armed with "authentic" maps—besieged the sisters for almost a century. But in 1957, when the hill was carved out for school expansion, no buried treasure surfaced. The sisters sold the grounds in 1980 to the American Film Institute.

6. CAHUENGA PASS
CAHUENGA BOULEVARD AND HIGHLAND AVENUE, HOLLYWOOD

In 1861 three Mexican government agents came north with $200,000 in gold, silver and jewelry to buy guns for the democracy struggle of Benito Juarez. For safe-keeping they buried the valuables in the hills of San Mateo.

A shepherd named Diego Moreno observed the men. After they left, Moreno dug up six packages and fled to Los Angeles. He stopped at a tavern near Cahuenga Pass and supposedly buried his stolen treasure under an ash tree.

Continuing into town, Moreno took ill and went to his friend Jesus Martinez. To repay Martinez for his kindness, Moreno told him about the fortune. After Moreno died, Martinez went treasure-hunting with his stepson, Gumisindo Correa. As Martinez found the tree, he dropped dead. His stepson, believing the treasure cursed, ran away.

A quarter-century later, a Basque shepherd supposedly unearthed one parcel filled with gold coins and jewels after his dog began digging under a tree. Elated with his newfound wealth, he returned to his homeland in Spain. But as his ship began to dock, he stood on the rail, slipped into the sea and sank with the heavy treasure sewn into his clothes.

Gumisindo Correa became a respected Los Angeles lawman, overcame his fear of the treasure and decided to look for it again. But before he could start, he was shot

Los Angeles Times

down in the streets of Los Angeles.

In 1939, the county issued a permit for two mining engineers to dig for the reputed treasure in one of the Hollywood Bowl parking lots. Nothing was found.

Ft. Moore Hill in 1941, before it was divided to make room for the county courthouse at Hill and 1st streets.

7. FORT MOORE HILL
BOUND BY THE HOLLYWOOD FREEWAY, HILL STREET AND SUNSET BOULEVARD

For almost a century, treasure hunters with imaginations fired by the exploits of the conquistadors hunted for thousands of dollars in Spanish gold allegedly buried beneath the hill's dusty crust, the site of the first U.S. flag-raising in California. During the 1950s construction of the Hollywood and Pasadena freeway segments, power shovels exposed bones and coffins at the site of the old French Cemetery, and bottles and utensils bearing marks of antiquity, but no gold. Today, the Los Angeles Unified School District Board of Education sits atop a legendary cache.

■ **More on Ft. Moore Hill, see below.**

SOURCES: "On the Old West Coast" by Major Horace Bell; "A Guide to Treasure in California" by Thomas Penfield; "Where to Find Gold in Southern California" by James Klein.

The History of Ft. Moore Hill

The downtown site overlooking Sunset Boulevard from Grand Avenue has been known as Ft. Moore Hill, named for Army Capt. Benjamin Moore, who had taken a lance through the heart at the battle of San Pasqual in San Diego County during the Mexican-American War.

On July 4, 1847, the first U.S. flag was raised over the military fort. It stood for 30 years, but was never finished because the volunteer Mormon Battalion that built it was mustered out of the service.

One of Los Angeles' first two cemeteries sat between crests on the hill, perhaps inspiring the Spanish name for the place—Canada de Los Muertos, or Ravine of the Dead.

Reading, writing and arithmetic came to Ft. Moore Hill in 1887, with the building of Central High School, later Central Junior High.

By 1901, the fort was gone, and the city started to build the concrete and brick

The Los Angeles Unified School District building, framed by the Hollywood Freeway, lower left; Hill Street, bottom right, and Sunset Boulevard, center.

Larry Davis / Los Angeles Times

Broadway Tunnel through the hill. Ten years later, construction began on the Pacific Electric tunnel that carried the old Red Cars through the hill between Hill Street and Grand Avenue.

As the city expanded westward, the hill began to lose prominence. Still, it was a place where commuters could park their cars for a nickel. After dark, lovers parked beneath the pepper trees.

In 1933, Ft. Moore Hill bounced back into the public eye with persistent rumors that thousands of dollars in Spanish gold was buried beneath its dusty crust.

City officials struck a bargain with treasure hunters—a 50-50 split of whatever they found. Spurred on by dreams of wealth, the gold diggers wound up with little more than rivulets of sweat dripping from their brows.

Reluctant to go away empty-handed, city officials tried to auction the 230,000 cubic yards of dirt shoveled out of the hill. A dirt-cheap bid of $11 came from a cynical fellow, who was ordered by the city to cart off the dirt and dump it where Union Station now stands.

In 1941, the hill was divided to make room for the county courthouse at Hill and 1st streets, built at a cost of $2 million. Five years later, the 700 Central Junior High students said their goodbyes and the school board moved into the red brick schoolhouse.

But more changes were still to come. The Broadway Tunnel was removed in 1944 to make way for the Hollywood Freeway. Most of the 1.4 million cubic yards of dirt excavated in the process was used to create an instant mini-mountain, covered with trees and shrubs, in Elysian Park.

Today, the two-story red brick schoolhouse is the meeting room for the Los Angeles Unified School District Board of Education. Its parking lot now covers what was once the cemetery, but a handful of old-timers can remember the tombs behind the boys' gym.

In 1967, part of the Pacific Electric Tunnel was removed to allow expansion of the school district building. About 100 yards of the tunnel still remain and are used as a depository for school board records.

On Hill, just north of Temple Street, what once was a waterfall cascading from the hill's crest is high and dry—a victim of the energy crisis and government economies. At the base of the old falls, though, interested passers-by can find the Ft. Moore Pioneer Memorial Monument.

Historic Churches

L.A. is rich in historic houses of worship
with exquisite or unusual architecture.

1. CHATSWORTH COMMUNITY CHURCH (1903)
OAKWOOD MEMORIAL PARK, 22601 LASSEN ST., CHATSWORTH

The oldest Protestant church in the San Fernando Valley sits on a cemetery knoll. It features a picturesque bell tower and classic New England church architecture. It originally stood at Topanga Boulevard near Devonshire Street, and Western film stars Roy Rogers and Dale Evans were active members in the 1940s and 1950s. In 1965, after it was sold to the Chatsworth Historical Society, the church was moved to a private cemetery. The congregation of St. Mary the Virgin Anglican Catholic Episcopal Church took up residence in the 75-seat building in 1981.

2. CHURCH OF THE ANGELS (1889)
1100 AVENUE 64, PASADENA

This Episcopal church was erected as a memorial to British-born California landowner Alexander Robert Campbell-Johnston by his widow, Frances, in 1889. Designed by two British architects, it is set in a three-acre garden in a part of town once known as Garvanza, a name adapted from the garbanzo sweet pea. The church

The Church of the Angels in Pasadena was built in 1889.

J. Albert Diaz / Los Angeles Times

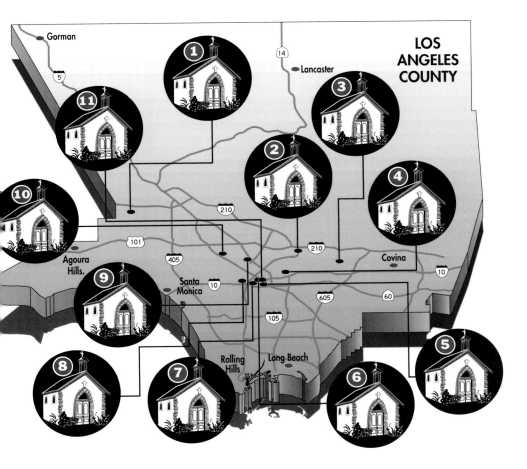

is built of sandstone hauled from quarries in the San Fernando Valley. A carved marble angel near the main entrance was a gift from construction workers.

3. CHURCH OF OUR SAVIOUR (1868)
535 W. ROSES ROAD, SAN GABRIEL

The oldest Protestant church in the San Gabriel Valley, this was also the first Episcopal church in Southern California. It features a post-World War II addition of a stained-glass window depicting a soldier in a tank, and a bronze statue of a uniformed soldier stands in the courtyard. The unique testaments are to Gen. George S. Patton, whose family helped build the church.

4. CHURCH OF THE EPIPHANY (1889)
2808 ALTURA ST., LINCOLN HEIGHTS

An architectural jewel, this Episcopal church is in the middle of one of the city's first suburbs. Stone buttresses support a single gabled roof dominated by a large round window. The sparse interior houses a vintage organ with delicately hand-painted pipes.

5. NISHI (HOMPA) HONGWANJI BUDDHIST TEMPLE (1925)
355-369 E. 1ST ST., LOS ANGELES

The oldest Buddhist temple in Los Angeles, this landmark brick building stands in the heart of Little Tokyo. It was built by some of Los Angeles' first Japanese immigrants after three Buddhist churches merged, forming a 2,000-member congregation. The front of the temple on Central Avenue has a mix of Asian and Egyptian motifs. During World War II, it was a storehouse for the belongings of many of the Japanese Americans who were interned in camps. Now it is home to the Japanese American National Museum.

6. PLAZA CHURCH (1862)
535 N. MAIN ST., LOS ANGELES

The Mission-style Roman Catholic church, near Olvera Street in the center of old downtown, is the city's oldest church. Construction funds were raised by auctioning seven barrels of brandy donated by the padres and 1,000 head of cattle. The original adobe structure was designed by Franciscan fathers and built by Native Americans in 1822. It was rebuilt in the Mission style in 1862. Its distinctive bell tower was erected in 1875, and the church itself was restored and enlarged in 1912.

7. SECOND BAPTIST CHURCH (1925)
2412 GRIFFITH AVE., LOS ANGELES

From humble beginnings in a stable near the old downtown plaza near present-day Olvera Street, the church has been a significant force in the black community since its founding in 1885. The building was designed in the Lombard Romanesque style by Norman Marsh, who designed Abbott Kinney's Venice development, and by African-American architect Paul R. Williams, who also designed Saks Fifth Avenue in Beverly Hills and the Beverly Hills Hotel.

8. WELSH PRESBYTERIAN CHURCH (1909)
1153 S. VALENCIA ST., LOS ANGELES

The first home of the Sinai Temple, the building became the Welsh Presbyterian Church when the synagogue moved in 1925. Still visible are the stars of David carved in stone in the side of the building. The Jewish congregation also left behind the original organ.

9. ANGELUS TEMPLE (1922)
1100 GLENDALE BLVD., ECHO PARK

In the 1920s and 1930s, evangelist Aimee Semple McPherson preached her Foursquare Gospel within this circular building. Its design is based on the Mormon Tabernacle in Salt Lake City. McPherson once explained that she was led by the Lord to the site "facing the entrance of peaceful Echo Park."
■ More on the "Saga of Sister Aimee," see Page 105.

Today the Angelus Temple is the headquarters of the International Foursquare Gospel Church.

Michael Edwards / Los Angeles Times

10. VEDANTA TEMPLE (1938)
1946 VEDANTA PLACE, HOLLYWOOD

The temple's fanciful facade features three onion-shaped domes topped with golden spires. In 1901, developer William Mead purchased four acres here as a rural retreat. Before he died in 1929, he deeded his property to the Vedanta Society of Southern California, founded as part of the older Ramakrishna Order of India. The temple is referred to by some as the "Little Taj."

11. ST. VIBIANA'S
2ND AND MAIN STREETS, LOS ANGELES

The Roman Catholic cathedral, mother church for the 3.5 million Catholics in the region, was modeled after the Church of San Miguel del Mar in Barcelona and built in 1876, when Los Angeles was a town of 9,000 residents. St. Vibiana's was named after and contains the relics of a 3rd-century maiden martyr, whose remains were unearthed in Italy in 1853 and brought to Los Angeles. Today, the Spanish-style cathedral is condemned, its coffin nails pounded down by the earthquake of 1994. Crippled and decaying, the fate of the downtown landmark is not certain.
■ More on St. Vibiana's, see Page 108.

The Saga of Sister Aimee

The city's reputation as the center of spiritual showmanship began on New Year's Day, 1923, at the dedication of the Angelus Temple overlooking Echo Park Lake.

An immense concrete building, with twin broadcasting towers and a revolving cross rimmed in neon lights perched on a domed roof, opened its doors on that day. It soon became world famous as the spiritual and theatrical base for the flamboyant Pentecostal evangelist Aimee Semple McPherson.

Aimee Semple
McPherson in
1935.

It was designed like a Broadway theater. Tiered rows of 5,300 seats dropped to the orchestra pit, where a young Anthony Quinn once played saxophone in the temple's band, and then to the stage where Sister Aimee sat on a red-velvet-cushioned chair.

To the sound of Sister Aimee's golden voice was added music from the temple's 30-foot golden organ; behind it all was a mural of Jesus with his hands outstretched toward Sister Aimee's flock.

The Canadian-born Aimee Kennedy received her calling when she was 18 years old, at a revival meeting in Canada. She wrote that she gave herself to Christ in response to the preaching of Robert Semple, an Irish Pentecostalist she married.

Two years later, Semple died of dysentery in Hong Kong, where they had gone as missionaries. Aimee returned to America with a baby daughter and married Harold (Mack) McPherson, a solid, unglamorous accountant with whom she had a son.

The honeymoon was soon over, and Aimee decided her mission was to preach. Mack wanted no part of a preacher's life and took off. The honey-haired Aimee barely noticed.

So she, her children and her iron-willed mother, Minnie (Ma) Kennedy, hit the road with $100, leaving Philadelphia in an Oldsmobile and showing up in the promised land of Los Angeles in 1918.

She started receiving attention after she donned a leather cap with goggles and scattered religious leaflets from an airplane. She held revival meetings at the Los Angeles Philharmonic Hall and in tents. Such a flair for showmanship drew huge crowds.

In a city whose roots were new and fragile, whose residents flocked here by the hundreds, Sister Aimee's faith promised a new and striking Los Angeles tradition. Her upbeat spiritualism—a blend of entertainment, religious faith and booster-ism—would lead many Angelenos through the Depression.

From the Jazz Age to World War II, she would be as famous and popular as any movie star, delivering a good show and sermon. She once compared Jesus Christ to the Lone Ranger, and once drove—dressed as a cop—onto the church stage on a motorcycle. "Stop!" she cried to the faithful. "You're speeding to ruin."

And she was as effective at raising money as she was at saving souls.

She would tell her Sabbath crowds: "I have a disease, an incurable disease. It is aggravated by the clinking of metal, but the rustle of that green stuff soothes it!" She was also known to instruct her congregation of 30,000 at collection time: "Sister has a headache tonight. Just quiet money, please."

As the collection plates filled up with money, so did the "miracle room" fill up with the crutches and wheelchairs of the healed. Her claims to miraculous healing brought in thousands, some of them suffering from incurable diseases, but many more hoping to witness firsthand the miracle cures. One 10-year-old victim of polio carried his shoes with him when he was brought up to her, confident that he would walk again—and he did.

She soon extended her reach beyond the lakefront church. A year after the temple was opened, Sister Aimee began broadcasting "The Sunshine Hour" every morning over radio station KFSG, which stood for Kalling Foursquare Gospel, the name of her church.

It was the radio station that proved her downfall—or rather the radio station's onetime engineer, a married man named Kenneth Ormiston.

On May 18, 1926, Sister Aimee, then 36, disappeared while swimming at Venice Beach. Hundreds knelt on the beach for days, praying and scanning the horizon for her. One young man shouted that he was going after her, plunged into the sea and drowned.

Sister Aimee resurfaced 36 days later in Douglas, Ariz., telling a harrowing tale of kidnap by "Jake," "Rose" and "Steve." Sister Aimee returned triumphantly to Los Angeles, where 100,000 people lined the streets to greet her rose-draped car.

Her followers believed her but authorities did not. They took Sister Aimee to court for "criminal (conspiracy) to commit acts injurious to public morals and to prevent and obstruct justice."

For months, the burning question in a Los Angeles courtroom was whether Aimee Semple McPherson had been kidnapped as she claimed, or had she run off to Carmel with Ormiston.

Authorities never found Jake, Steve or Rose. They suspected Sister Aimee had a tryst with an engineer on her radio station—and had tried to cover up for her absence by her vanishing act off Venice Beach and her "miraculous" reappearance.

But despite the lurid court hearings, with evidence of a clandestine rendezvous in a Carmel motel and allegations of a cover-up, the charges were dropped by the district attorney.

Sister Aimee called the scandal a plot hatched by the devil, and she embarked on a "Vindication Tour."

Although the faithful kept coming, her reputation was blemished and her popularity with the public and press began to fade.

In 1944, Sister Aimee died of a barbiturate overdose while touring Oakland. Her body was brought back to Los Angeles, and more than 40,000 mourners prayed at her coffin. She was dressed in the white dress and a gray-lined navy cloak that had become a spiritual uniform. She was succeeded as president by her son, Rolf McPherson. He retired in 1988.

Sister Aimee, a charismatic lightning rod, gained fame and fortune from her ability to denounce sin in entertaining ways. She was a pioneer who blazed a trail for other women ministers and established 411 Foursquare Gospel churches in the United States, half of which were run by women ministers.

Today, the Angelus Temple, headquarters of the International Church of the Foursquare Gospel, has grown to 1.73 million members at 25,300 churches and meeting sites worldwide.

The church celebrates Oct. 9, Sister Aimee's birthday, as Founder's Day.

St. Vibiana's Cathedral

For more than a century, St. Vibiana's Cathedral has dominated this city's religious profile, enduring troubles inside the building and out.

Over the years, the old Baroque Spanish-style brick building—the center of the nation's most populous Roman Catholic archdiocese—has been ravaged by trespassers' fires and threatened over and again with demolition.

In the 1860s, Los Angeles was a little town with fewer than 5,700 residents, but 3,000 of them were Catholic, and they had big aspirations. The church offered to build them a cathedral.

It was modeled after the Church of San Miguel del Mar in Barcelona, Spain. Construction began at 2nd and Main Streets in 1872, but came to a halt when the diocese ran out of money. After a few more fund-raisers, builders Louis Mesmer and his son Joseph were brought in. "Employing every bricklayer that can be found in the city," according to an account at the time, they completed the work in January, 1876, at a cost of $80,000.

There was never a doubt what name the cathedral would bear. In 1853, when Los Angeles Bishop Thaddeus Amat was in Rome, a skeleton had been unearthed amid the catacombs. They were the relics of St. Vibiana, an obscure 3rd-century maiden martyr, and Pope Pius IX asked Amat to take her remains to California and build a cathedral in her name.

Ten years after the cathedral was dedicated and St. Vibiana's relics were in place, a new bishop, Francis Mora, built a three-story brick schoolhouse behind the cathedral. The elementary school was run by the Immaculate Heart Sisters.

By the turn of the century, however, the diocese thought it had outgrown St. Vibiana's. In 1904, Bishop Thomas J. Conaty proposed an immense domed cathedral on 9th Street and received papal permission to tear down St. Vibiana's.

That effort failed, but four decades later "St. Vib's," as the church is often called, seemed doomed again. Archbishop John J. Cantwell, who publicly equated the cathedral with "worn-out garments," unveiled plans for new, block-long, $1.5-million mother church on Wilshire Boulevard.

But Cantwell's health failed before his dream could be realized. The new diocesan leader, Cardinal James Francis McIntyre, scrubbed the plans in order to devote the church's money to elementary schools.

McIntyre began in 1948 by knocking down the old red brick schoolhouse, where many naughty youths had carved their initials in windowsills. Left behind by the wrecking ball were scraps of paper: a writing lesson by a boy named Ernest: "School will be fun. School will be fun." And a girl named Marie's inconsistent arithmetic: "5 plus 4 equals 9; 4 plus 5 equals 8." There was an unsigned note, too, on stationery decorated with hearts and Xs. It read: "Will you meet me at recess?"

A more modern school was built on the site, but shut down in the early 1980s because of dwindling attendance. At the same time, the homeless scattered about the area were becoming a problem and the church's doors had to remain locked. Indeed, much of the scenery around St. Vibiana's was declining.

Through the years, the cathedral has stood as a silent witness to joy and pain: thousands of baptisms and weddings, many funerals and a few tragedies. In 1921, the distraught editor of a journal called Reason, published by her father, the Rev. B.F. Austin, shot and killed herself in the cathedral's vestibule.

St. Vibiana's
Cathedral is
surrounded by
the skyline of
downtown Los
Angeles.

Ken Lubas / Los Angeles Times

A burglar bled to death in the courtyard in 1948 after he cut his arm on the
window he had broken trying to get into the church.

Later, trespassers set fire to its interior and rifled the poor boxes.

Offbeat Museums

Unusual museums with specialties ranging from bananas to brassieres offer a variety of unexpected treasures.

1. MUSEUM OF RADIO & TELEVISION
465 N. BEVERLY DR., BEVERLY HILLS

The 23,000-square-foot archive is an offshoot of the original museum in New York. The museum has 75,000 clips of TV and radio programs and advertising spots that the public can view or hear. There's a wide range, from President Franklin Roosevelt's fireside radio chats to episodes of "I Love Lucy." Admission is $6 for adults and $4 for senior citizens and students. (310) 786-1000.

2. INTERNATIONAL BRASSIERE MUSEUM
6608 HOLLYWOOD BLVD., HOLLYWOOD

Frederick's of Hollywood, the lingerie vendor, has set aside a portion of its Hollywood Boulevard store as the International Brassiere Museum, featuring specimens believed to have had "far-reaching effect" on the development of the undergarment as an art object. Visitors will find the first dress worn on television by comic Milton Berle, pantaloons from Ava Gardner, a slip from Lana Turner, a nightgown from Judy Garland, a peignoir worn by Mae West and Madonna's bustier, which miraculously reappeared after it was stolen during the 1992 riots. Hours: 10 a.m. to 6:45 p.m. Monday through Thursday, 10 a.m. to 9:45 p.m. Friday, 10 a.m. to 6 p.m. Saturday and noon to 5 p.m. Sunday. Admission is free. (213) 466-8506.

3. BANANA MUSEUM
2524 EL MOLINO AVE., ALTADENA

A top-banana photographer and photo-equipment salesman named Ken Bannister shows off his 15,000 banana-shaped treasures, ranging from a banana purse, a banana sequined with an image of Michael Jackson, banana umbrella, pup tent, puppets, golf putter and a movie poster of "Herbie Goes Bananas." The museum is open to members of the International Banana Club and guests by appointment only. (818) 798-2272.

4. AMERICAN SOCIETY OF PATRIOTIC HISTORY MUSEUM
1918 N. ROSEMEAD BLVD., SOUTH EL MONTE

Don Michelson, an officer in the Quartermaster Corps during World War II, and his son, Craig, work every day at breathing new life into old weapons at their

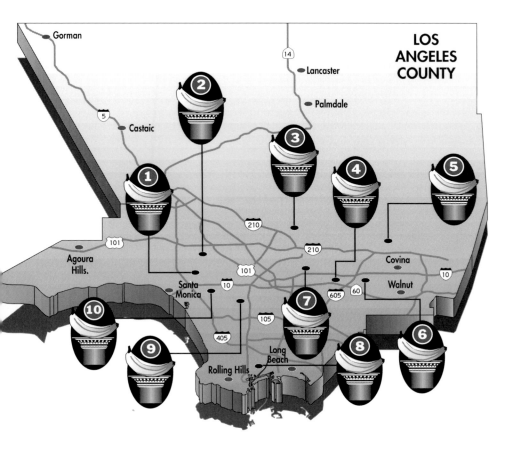

Army camp-like museum. At the 7 1/2-acre outdoor display that resembles a staging area for an invasion, visitors will find Jeeps, trucks, ambulances, self-propelled anti-tank guns, war uniforms and 30-ton Sherman tanks. The museum loans out its drivable tanks and trucks to the American Legion and other groups to use in parades. Open on dry weekends from noon to 4:30 p.m. Admission is $3. (818) 442-1776.

5. SEDLY PECK MEMORIAL MUSEUM
23400 E. FORK ROAD, FOLLOWS CAMP, AZUSA

Sedley Peck, born in 1889, was often called the "mayor of Azusa Canyon" in deference to his popularity among canyon residents and his trunk full of notes, mementos, clippings and photographs that recounted the rich saga of the San Gabriel Canyon. The museum, which displays much of Peck's mining memorabilia, is in the Henry C. Roberts store, the oldest building in the San Gabriel Mountains. Take California 39 about 17 miles from the Azusa turnoff on the Foothill Freeway

(210) and then turn east, or right, to East Fork Road for another three miles. Open on weekends by appointment only. (818) 910-1100.

6. RALPH W. MILLER GOLF LIBRARY AND MUSEUM
1 INDUSTRY HILLS PARKWAY, CITY OF INDUSTRY

Guests at the Industry Hills Sheraton Resort are often surprised to find the Ralph W. Miller Golf Library and Museum. The library collection offers more than 5,000 volumes on the science and history of the game, including a 1597 edition of "Laws and Actes of Parliament," recording the edict of 1495 that banned Scots from playing golf because Scottish lords felt that people should be learning archery to defend their lands rather than hitting balls. The museum's memorabilia includes score cards, postcards, medals, art work, a tee collection, golf ball exhibit, Babe Didrikson Zaharias' golf knickers and golf bags, and the clubs of Bobby Jones, Craig Woods, Amy Alcott and other famous players. Hours: 9 a.m. to 6:30 p.m. Tuesday through Friday and noon to 4 p.m. Saturday and Sunday. Closed Monday. (818) 854-2354.

7. RAMONA CONVENT SCHOOL MUSEUM
1701 W. RAMONA ROAD, ALHAMBRA

Ramona Convent is the most visible landmark in the city of Alhambra and is said to be the oldest private Catholic school in Los Angeles County still on its original site. For more than 107 years the school has stood on a hill while the surrounding area has been transformed from open ranch land to urban sprawl. Visitors can trace the school and area's growth at this free, historic exhibit of photos and artifacts. Open Monday through Friday 8 a.m. to 4 p.m. by appointment only. (818) 282-4151.

8. DRUM BARRACKS CIVIL WAR MUSEUM AND LIBRARY
1052 BANNING BLVD., WILMINGTON

The museum and library are housed in what is the last remaining major building from Camp Drum on a 60-acre training compound, which served as headquarters for Union commanders and is the only intact U.S. Army building from the Civil War period in Southern California. Visitors can learn about the period through theatrical skits. Fierce, drawn-out battles are re-enacted with miniatures, while costumed performers re-enact traditions and demonstrate crafts and dances. Its library boasts a complete set of the National Archives' "Official Records of the War of the Rebellion," documenting just about every detail of life in the Union and Confederate armies and navies. (310) 548-7509.

9. EARTHMOBILE
LOS ANGELES COUNTY NATURAL HISTORY MUSEUM,
900 EXPOSITION BLVD., LOS ANGELES

Third- through sixth-graders can become archeologists, digging in desert sand for planted "artifacts" in a make-believe Southwestern canyon. The canyon is inside a 48-foot air-conditioned truck called the "Earthmobile." In a time when schools can rarely afford field trips, this traveling museum brings the great outdoors right onto the playground. Schools in the Los Angeles Unified School District can call (213) 744-3520 to make reservations.

Ken Hively / Los Angeles Times

Exhibits that illuminate the offbeat are featured at the Museum of Jurassic Technology.

10. THE MUSEUM OF JURASSIC TECHNOLOGY
9341 VENICE BLVD., LOS ANGELES

Visitors expecting dinosaurs will instead be confronted with a quirky display devoted to the radar-equipped Deprong Mori bat, a horn that grew from a woman's head, a diorama of a rain forest where crazed stink ants cling to vines and the incessant barking of a coyote head. The brainchild of former movie miniaturist David Wilson, this museum's exhibits illuminate arcane subjects, among them notions that traditional science has laughed at, rejected or refused to acknowledge. Hours: 2 to 8 p.m. Thursdays, noon to 6 p.m. Friday through Sunday. Admission is $3 and $2 for senior citizens and students. Call (310) 836-6131.

Offbeat Libraries

Little-known libraries offer information on subjects from plants and family roots to racing and nudists.

---

1. ELYSIUM NUDIST & NATURIST ARCHIVES
814 ROBINSON ROAD, TOPANGA CANYON

This special library, surrounded by eight lush acres, reflects the vision and passion of the book-publishing empire of the late Ed Lange, founder of the nonprofit Elysium Fields, L.A. County's only nudist colony. Lange left a collection of more than 10,000 still photos and hundreds of books and magazines that date to the 1920s. Open by appointment only. Call Chris Moran at (310) 455-1000.

2. CALIFORNIA FILM COMMISSION LOCATION LIBRARY
6922 HOLLYWOOD BLVD., SUITE 600, HOLLYWOOD

Catering to the needs of the film industry, brides looking for a glamorous, fairy-tale wedding site and special-event planners, the commission has more than 300,000 photographs of locations statewide. The files are organized by subject and region and include books, maps, brochures and a database with more than 7,000 names of location contacts. Open from 8 a.m. to 6 p.m. Monday through Friday. Residents who want to list their property can call the library at (213) 736-2855.

The Academy of Motion Picture Arts & Sciences Library in Beverly Hills stocks more than 8,000 movie and television show scripts.

3. PACIFICA RADIO ARCHIVES
3729 CAHUENGA BLVD., NORTH HOLLYWOOD

Since 1959, the oldest collection of public radio programming in the country has been housed at the progressive radio station KPFK-FM, committed to freedom of expression. Built from the tape collection of the five radio stations of the Pacifica Foundation, the library maintains more than 40,000 documentary tapes of historical events. Visitors and mail-order clients can listen to recordings that include Watergate and Iran-Contra hearings, talks by linguist Noam Chomsky and feminist Gloria Steinem, music by jazz great Duke Ellington, Malcolm X speeches and the oral memoirs of the crew that dropped the first atomic bomb. The library is free to visitors, but there is a small fee for mail-order tapes. Open 9 a.m. to 5 p.m. Monday through Friday. For access to the library through the World Wide Web, the address is: http://www.igc.apc.org/pacifica. Or call (818) 506-1077.

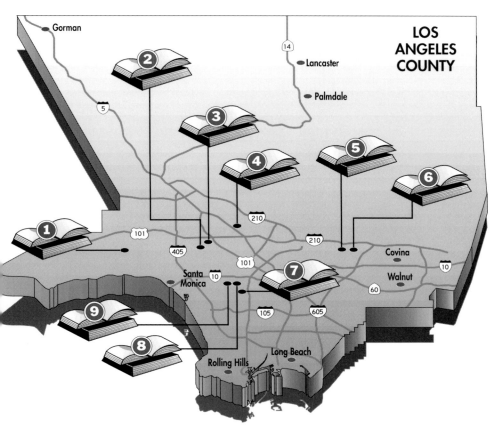

4. SOUTHERN CALIFORNIA GENEALOGICAL SOCIETY

122 S. SAN FERNANDO BLVD., BURBANK

If you are interested in digging up family roots and knowing whether your forebears arrived on the Mayflower or if you are descended from royalty, here's a good place to start. Volunteer genealogists offer classes and will help direct your research, beginning with a pedigree chart of your family history. Open 10 a.m. to 4 p.m. Monday through Saturday, 10 a.m. to 9 p.m. Tuesday and 10 a.m. to 4 p.m. Sunday, but closed the third Sunday of the month. (818) 843-7247.

For a collection of German genealogies, try the Immigrants Library in North Hollywood. The Sons of the Revolution Library in Glendale deals predominantly with the Revolutionary War period, but has a Civil War section. More extensive records on genealogy and classes to help researchers can be found at the Mormon Temple History Center on Santa Monica Boulevard in West Los Angeles.

5. PLANT SCIENCE LIBRARY
LOS ANGELES COUNTY AND STATE ARBORETUM,
301 BALDWIN AVE., ARCADIA

Gardening enthusiasts and landscape designers can reap a harvest of help from horticulturists and botanists at the Southern California plant science, 26,000-volume library open to the public. Would-be herbalists can study one of the library's oldest books, "A Newe Herball, or Historie of Plants," published in 1578, to learn about plants used to treat ailments during the time of Queen Elizabeth I. Open 9 a.m. to 4:30 p.m. Monday through Friday. (818) 821-3222.

6. CARLETON F. BURKE MEMORIAL LIBRARY
201 COLORADO PLACE, ARCADIA

Gamblers on their way to play the ponies at Santa Anita Park can pick a historic winner at the California Horse Racing Hall of Fame, a museum and library located in the headquarters of the California Thoroughbred Breeders Assn. It houses racing chart books from the early 1900s, and decades of the Daily Racing Form's West Coast edition. More than 10,000 horse-related volumes, microfiche files and periodicals are used not only by gamblers, but also to study genetic lines to plan horse matings. The library is named for a late Santa Anita racing official and a leader of California racing, whose collection evolved into the library. Free to the public from 9 a.m. to 4 p.m. Monday through Friday. (818) 445-7800.

7. SOUTHERN CALIFORNIA LIBRARY FOR SOCIAL STUDIES AND RESEARCH
6120 S. VERMONT AVE., LOS ANGELES

This unique institution, founded in 1963, documents the history of social movements in the West and was started by Emil Freed, a well-known labor organizer, avowed Communist and local activist. The library's documents trace local episodes such as the Hollywood studio strikes of the 1940s and the work of the L.A. Committee for the Protection of the Foreign-Born, which fought political deportations from the '40s through the '60s. Freed's books, documentary films, pamphlets, magazines and photographs from the '20s make up much of the library's holdings. Open 10 a.m. to 4 p.m. Tuesday through Saturday. (213) 759-6063.

8. PAUL ZIFFREN SPORTS CENTER LIBRARY
AMATEUR ATHLETIC FOUNDATION,
2141 W. ADAMS BLVD., LOS ANGELES

Scholars and browsers visiting the nation's largest sports library can view treasures dating to the 19th century: professional and collegiate basketball media guides and game programs, and books and magazines on outdoor sports such as hunting and fishing, and on bullfighting. There is also an index of 175,000 sports personalities, facilities and events, with another 1.5 million references to a news clipping file. The library was named for the former chairman of the board of the Los Angeles Olympic Organizing Committee. Open from 10 a.m. to 5 p.m. Monday, Tuesday, Thursday and Friday; 10 a.m. to 8:30 p.m. Wednesday, and 10 a.m. to 3 p.m. on even-dated Saturdays. (213) 730-9696.

The Paul Ziffren Sports Center Library, at the Amateur Athletic Foundation on West Adams Boulevard, is the largest sports library in the country.

Al Seib / Los Angeles Times

9. WILLIAM ANDREWS CLARK MEMORIAL LIBRARY
2520 CIMARRON ST., LOS ANGELES

William Andrews Clark Jr., the founder of the Los Angeles Philharmonic Orchestra, bequeathed his home and library to UCLA when he died in 1934. The library was named for his father, a senator from Montana who made the family fortune in copper. The depository of English literature and history of the 17th, 18th and 19th centuries is open to serious researchers, Monday through Friday 9 a.m. to 5 p.m. (213) 731-8529.

NOTE: The Los Angeles County Public Library system includes four resource centers providing materials on different racial and ethnic groups: the Black Resource Center is in the A.C. Bilbrew Library in Los Angeles, the American Indian Resource Center is in the Huntington Park Library, the Asian Pacific Resource Center is in the Montebello Library and the Chicano Resource Center is in the East Los Angeles Library.

Book Nooks

From metaphysics to mysteries, L.A. abounds in bookstores catering to specialized interests.

1. ESO WON BOOKSHOP
900 N. LA BREA AVE., INGLEWOOD

Eso Won, the African name for the city of Aswan, Egypt, which means "water over rocks" in the Amharic language of Ethiopia, has become the cornerstone of L.A.'s burgeoning black literary scene. Smaller than the average mall bookstore, Eso Won is as dense and neatly sectioned as a library, though bright splashes of African decor and strains of jazz considerably soften the austerity. In addition, the store is known for regularly hosting readings and signings with authors. (310) 674-6566.

2. THE BODHI TREE
8585 MELROSE AVE., WEST HOLLYWOOD

The Bodhi hasn't changed much since the early 1970s. The aroma of incense drifts around the store and sitar music slices the air. Visitors can still relax and do their browsing in comfortable chairs. Customers peruse vegetarian diet guides, books on holistic healing and material dealing with a wide range of spiritual and philosophical issues. The store also offers non-book items ranging from bells and flutes to herbal toothpaste.

3. DUTTON'S BOOKS
5146 LAUREL CANYON BLVD., NORTH HOLLYWOOD

This well-established bookshop near the intersection of Laurel Canyon and Magnolia boulevards has a relaxed atmosphere. The building where Dutton's started in 1961 was in the Cape Cod Colonial style. Over the years the store has expanded twice into neighboring business spaces. Like living organisms, the books seemed to multiply and spread. Today they occupy shelves and cabinets in rooms of many shapes and sizes, including hallways, alcoves and a converted closet or two.

4. SPORTSBOOKS
8302 MELROSE AVE., WEST HOLLYWOOD

Starting a small, specialized retail bookstore in the 1990s shows all the optimism of a pint-size quarterback calling an "everybody go long" play on a muddy field at the city park. And about the same chance of success. But SportsBooks seems to have secured its niche, and owners John Berylson and Art Kaminsky still think

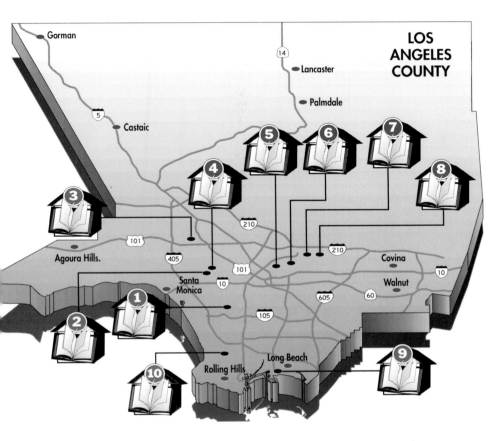

they can go all the way. They have drafted Wilt Chamberlain, John Wooden, W.P. Kinsella and Roger Kahn over the years. SportsBooks features current books, magazines, memorabilia and collectibles.

5. BOOK 'EM
1118 MISSION ST., SOUTH PASADENA

A center for mystery buffs, Book 'Em had only been open about a year when a fire destroyed the original South Pasadena location in the fall of 1991. The bookstore reopened a short distance down Mission Street not long after. Along with mystery and suspense titles are reference books on the genre, a juvenile section and a fair number of contemporary horror novels. Book 'Em puts strong emphasis on support for local authors, with autographing sessions by Steve Allen, Jonathan Kellerman, Faye Kellerman and Robert K. Tanenbaum among others.

Pacific Asia Museum bookstore is part of a cultural center featuring books on the arts, philosophy and history of Asia and Pacific islands.

George Rose / Los Angeles Times

6. PACIFIC ASIA MUSEUM
46 N. LOS ROBLES AVE., PASADENA

This shop is the only one in Greater Los Angeles housed in an example of Chinese Imperial Palace architecture, with a traditional courtyard garden and koi pond outside. Part of a cultural center featuring galleries, classrooms, an auditorium and a library, the store offers books on the art, philosophy, history and literature of Asia and the Pacific islands. Atop the ornately curved eaves and green roof tiles stand two ceramic "guardian dogs" watching for enemies, while giant stone *fo* dogs, resembling lions, protect the courtyard.

7. MITCHELL BOOKS
71395 E. WASHINGTON BLVD., PASADENA

The 1930s brick building where this shop's recessed doorway is found is a perfect setting for another shop specializing in mystery fiction—first editions, rare books and used hardcover and softcover volumes. It is the nation's largest dealer in out-of-print mystery and crime books. One expects to see a Bogey look-alike in a tan trenchcoat pull aside the curtain of the second-floor apartment window above. Inside, behind the Venetian blinds hanging in the front windows, the store is narrow and deep. Far back in narrow aisles beneath old film posters are 19th-century novels by Wilkie Collins and the latest by Sue Grafton. The mass-market paperbacks are only slightly alphabetized and the stock may be a little dusty, but there are treasures.

8. SAN MARINO TOY & BOOK SHOPPE
2424 HUNTINGTON DR., SAN MARINO

This store stands apart for its focus on books, toys, games, recordings and all manner of material for children from infancy to the teen years, as well as on books on parenting. This is a proactive bookstore, from its knowledgeable clerks to its sponsorship of school book fairs to its efforts to bring to town such authors as Jim Trelease ("The Read-Aloud Handbook") and recording artists popular with kids, such as Canadian singer and guitarist Raffi ("Baby Beluga").

Acres of Books has 6.5 miles of shelves to accommodate all the titles.

9. ACRES OF BOOKS
240 LONG BEACH BLVD., LONG BEACH

This is the Big One. Estimates of the number of books at Smith's Acres of Books range from half a million to 750,000. They take up 6.5 miles of shelving. For nearly 30 years, Acres of Books has been in a building of the Streamline Moderne architectural style. A couple of years back, the City Council voted to make it a cultural heritage landmark. Formerly a country-music dance hall, it has horseshoes imprinted in the concrete at one entrance and a 20-foot-wide Western painting that hovers over the books. The fiction room grows so dark on overcast days that flashlights are loaned to customers.

10. STEP'N STONES
1327 POST AVE., TORRANCE

This shop's owners claim it is the nation's largest self-help and recovery-program bookstore, offering more than 3,000 book titles and 1,000 audio and video-tapes dealing with topics ranging from motivation and self-esteem to addictions and dysfunctional relationships.

City of Angles

Architectural zaniness—funky landmarks like the old Brown Derby—remains a vital part of our cityscape.

----

1. CHIAT DAY ADVERTISING AGENCY
340 MAIN ST., VENICE

Completed in 1991, the 75,000-square-foot building designed by noted L.A. architect Frank Gehry has as its entry a three-story, upright pair of binoculars. The eyepieces serve as skylights illuminating the interior of the binoculars, which open into a large conference room. To enter the building's underground garage, cars must drive between the upright lenses.

2. THE DUTCH CASTLE
1366 ANGELO DR., BEVERLY HILLS

Also known as Kasteel Kamphuyzen, the 6,000-square-foot main house and 1,600-square-foot gatehouse are perched on the edge of a canyon in Beverly Hills. The castle was built in 1981 by Beverly Hills designer Mark Nixon and named for his business partner, Baron Herbert Hischemoeller van Kamphuyzen of the Netherlands. The structures, with stepped gables inspired by the 16th-century castles and townhouses of Holland, have been the scene of many civic, corporate and charitable galas.

3. THE WITCH'S COTTAGE
CARMELITA AVENUE AND WALDEN DRIVE, BEVERLY HILLS

The storybook house was built in Culver City in 1921 but moved eight years later to its present location because of traffic problems caused by gawkers. It was designed by art director Harry C. Oliver, who won an Oscar for design with "Seventh Heaven" and invented a machine that creates fake cobwebs. Photo page 163.

4. MALIBU CASTLE
OVERLOOKING THE MALIBU CIVIC CENTER NEAR
WEBB WAY AND PACIFIC COAST HIGHWAY

This reproduction of a 13th-century Scottish castle was designed by a physician and constructed of man-made stones. It is visible from the Pacific Coast Highway. "Tattoo" was imprisoned here for an episode of "Fantasy Island"; James Garner hounded a rock star here in the "Rockford Files," and Toyota Celica drove around its brick-floored courtyard for a commercial.

Malibu Castle, visible from Pacific Coast Highway.

Mary Frampton / Los Angeles Times

5. TOWER OF WOODEN PALLETS
15357 MAGNOLIA BLVD., SHERMAN OAKS

Designated a city landmark in 1978, the tower was built in 1951 by Daniel Van Meter in his backyard from 2,000 platforms discarded by the Schlitz brewery.

6. TAIL O' THE PUP
SAN VICENTE BOULEVARD NEAR BEVERLY BOULEVARD, WEST HOLLYWOOD

Hidden behind the bulky Ma Maison Sofitel hotel, the steel-reinforced, 17-foot hot dog with mustard, designed in 1938 by Milton J. Black, lives on.

7. STONE GATES
BEACHWOOD, WESTSHIRE AND BELDEN DRIVES, LOS ANGELES

Built by European stonemasons in the early 1920s, the gates form the entrance to Hollywoodland, a residential subdivision that gave Los Angeles one of its best-known landmarks. As an advertising gimmick, a huge HOLLYWOODLAND sign was erected high in the hills. The last syllable was removed in 1946 because it was in

Tower of Wooden Pallets, a back-yard monument constructed from 2,000 discarded platforms.

Bob Carey / Los Angeles Times

poor condition.

8. CAPITOL RECORDS
1750 VINE ST., HOLLYWOOD

Reminiscent of a stack of 45-r.p.m. records with a stylus on top, the familiar office building, designed by Welton Becket in 1954, has become a symbol of the Hollywood skyline. Frank Sinatra was the first to use the recording studios when he conducted a 56-piece orchestra in February, 1956.

9. CROSSROADS OF THE WORLD
6671 SUNSET BLVD., LOS ANGELES

With its fantasy-like architecture by Robert Derrah, the Crossroads, which opened on Oct. 29, 1936, was Los Angeles' first cosmopolitan shopping mall. The central building is patterned after a ship on a world cruise, passing small shops representing a variety of architectural styles—Spanish Colonial, Tudor, French Provincial. Atop its 55-foot tower sits a giant revolving globe that for half a century has been one of Hollywood's most familiar beacons.

10. THE DARK ROOM
5370 WILSHIRE BLVD., LOS ANGELES

This replica of a Leica camera, complete with lens and shutter-speed indicator, was built in 1938 by architect Marcus P. Miller and originally served as a camera shop. Today, it houses Sher-e Punjab Cuisine, probably the only Indian restaurant in which customers enter through a camera. Sher-e means tiger.

11. MUSEUM OF NEON ART
501 W. OLYMPIC BLVD., LOS ANGELES

Better known by its acronym MONA, this neon museum is brightened by an Art Deco light-bulb lady once perched atop the Melrose Theater, where she'd held her urn of falling water since 1923.

12. TRIFORIUM
TEMPLE AND MAIN STREETS, LOS ANGELES

A three-booster shuttle held together by a multicolored plastic belt is actually a $900,000 municipal music box—programmed to play daily from 5:30 to 8:30 p.m.

13. DONUT HOLE
15300 AMAR ROAD, LA PUENTE

This drive-in doughnut shop was built in 1946 and resembles two gigantic chocolate doughnuts stuck together in a baker's box. Each hollow fiberglass doughnut is 26 feet in diameter. It has been featured in movies, including "Dragnet" and "Moving Violation," and in a German rock group's video.

14. OUR LADY OF GUADALUPE CHURCH
16239 ARROW HWY., IRWINDALE

Wedged between an auto shop and Morada Street, the tiny, 90-seat mission was built with thousands of rocks that were lifted from the San Gabriel River bed by neighbors 75 years ago.

Coca-Cola Bottling Co., nautical L.A. headquarters.

Ken Hively / Los Angeles Times

15. ROCK CASTLE
844 LIVE OAK AVE., GLENDORA

The gargantuan, 22,000-square-foot palace of stream-rolled rocks, cannons, parapets and six-foot cinder block walls is topped with barbed wire and a 74-foot clock tower that chimes the hours. The private residence was built by Michael Rubel in 1985.

16. COCA-COLA BOTTLING CO.
1334 SOUTH CENTRAL AVE., LOS ANGELES

Designed by Robert Derrah in 1936 and shaped like an 1890s-era ocean liner, this utilitarian structure is complete with porthole windows, ship doors, a promenade deck, catwalk and metal riveting. The nautical image was intended to connote coolness and cleanliness.

17. CHILI BOWLS
12244 W. PICO BLVD., WEST LOS ANGELES, AND
2230 E. FLORENCE AVE., WALNUT PARK

The slogan "We cook our beans backward—you only get the hiccups," was adopted by Arthur Whizin, who built the original 18 Chili Bowls in the early 1930s. Four still stand. Taking up space in the bowls are a body shop in Glendale, a bar in Walnut Park, a family restaurant in Los Angeles and a Chinese eatery in Montebello.

18. ASSYRIAN WALL
5675 E. TELEGRAPH ROAD, CITY OF COMMERCE

The former Uniroyal tire factory next to the Santa Ana Freeway, built in 1929 with a distinctive 1,700-foot-long facade, recalls the palace of Sargon II, an Assyrian king. It is now the Citadel, a discount shopping center.

19. ACADEMY THEATER
3100 MANCHESTER BLVD., INGLEWOOD

Built in 1939, this futuristic structure is distinguished by its pencil-like, 125-foot cylindrical tower, crowned with an optimistic sunburst.

Source: "California Crazy, Roadside Vernacular Architecture" by Jim Heimann and Rip Georges.

III.
WHO NEEDS DISNEYLAND?

U NIVERSAL CITY AND MAGIC MOUNTAIN MAY BE L.A. COUNTY'S ONLY big-ticket amusement parks, but recreational destinations abound. Indeed, in bounty and variety, L.A.'s leisure menu may exceed any other metroplex'. From virtual-reality thrills to scenic tranquillity, you'll find ample options in the following pages.

Some of our manifest delights need no documenting here: beaches for sunning and surfing, busy boardwalks and bikeways, nearby mountains for skiing and snow-boarding. Other pleasurable pastimes need publicizing. You can, for instance, learn to drag race (in Palmdale) or just simulate it (in Old Town Pasadena). You can bungee jump (in Azusa Canyon), make your own beer (at a do-it-yourself brewery in Hermosa Beach), watch a planetarium laser display (at Griffith Park Observa-tory). Many popular recreational resources are available all over the map—jogging and equestrian trails, petting zoos and wild-animal farms, mini-train rides (for kids and even pets), pluck-it-yourself orchards, exotic arboretums and elegant gardens.

And, of course, Disneyland is just down the freeway.

Animal Attractions

From canine playgrounds to rescue centers, L.A. County offers something for almost every animal lover.

1. LOS ANGELES PET MEMORIAL PARK
5068 N. OLD SCANDIA LANE, CALABASAS

This 10-acre literary landmark in the foothills of Calabasas was started in 1928 in the corner of a cattle-grazing range. Later, the pet cemetery became the "Happier Hunting Ground" in English author Evelyn Waugh's 1948 satirical novel, "The Loved One." It's now the final resting spot for about 40,000 animal best friends, from the obscure to the notable: Hopalong Cassidy's horse Topper, Humphrey Bogart's dog Droopy, Charlie Chaplin's cat Boots, Rudolph Valentino's dog Kabar, Tonto's steed Scout in "The Lone Ranger" and the speckled pooch Petey from "Our Gang." Open 8:30 a.m to 4:30 p.m. Monday through Saturday. Park open but office closed Sundays. (818) 591-7037.

Straddling the Gardena-Carson border sits Los Angeles County's other animal graveyard. Pet Haven, the final resting place for more than 30,000 animals, was created in 1948 by a pet owner who was upset that a lack of water in Calabasas prevented him from growing grass over his dog's grave there. Burial costs begin at $375 and cremation starts at $50. Open 7 a.m. to 3 p.m. weekdays, 9 a.m. to 1 p.m. Saturday and closed Sunday. (310) 532-2477.

2. GUIDE DOGS OF AMERICA
13445 GLENOAKS BLVD., SYLMAR

This 6 1/2-acre Sylmar school, which relies entirely on private donations, is one of 11 guide dog schools in the country. It was founded in 1948 by Joseph W. Jones, a blind machinist who had been denied a guide dog by the one school that existed at that time. Its officials decided that, at 59, he was too old for a guide dog. Here, golden and Labrador retrievers and German shepherds train for service to the blind. A free tour provides insight into dog care, breeding, training and housing for dogs and humans. Tours are available at 10 a.m. and 2 p.m. daily, but call first for reservations. (818) 362-5834.

3. WILDLIFE WAYSTATION
14831 LITTLE TUJUNGA CANYON ROAD, LAKE VIEW TERRACE

In a rugged, rocky canyon in the Angeles National Forest sits a 160-acre refuge for abandoned and abused animals, from crocodiles to cockatoos and bobcats to boa

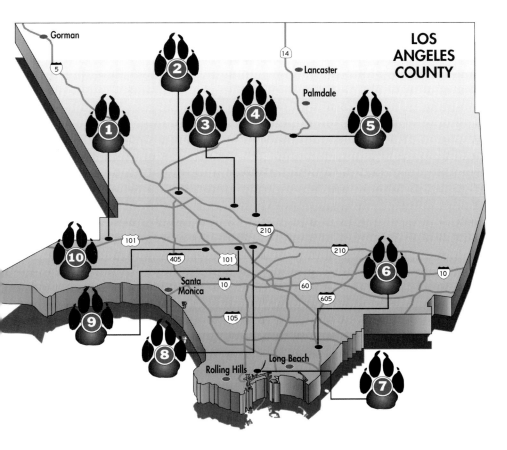

constrictors. More than 1,000 animals, forsaken by zoos or just needing a serene place to spend their final years, are cared for by a 15-member staff and 40 full-time and 175 part-time volunteers. Aside from educating the public about the needs of exotic and wild animals, the goal of the waystation—the only facility of its kind in the country—is to release into the wild those animals that can survive, and find homes for others. For information about volunteering or Sunday tours, (818) 899-5201.

4. WILDLIFE ON WHEELS
SUNLAND

When it's not roving, this perambulatory nonprofit storytelling and animal-awareness program is parked on a one-acre ranch populated by a variety of exotic animals—llamas, monkeys, alligators, wildcats, foxes and an American bald eagle. The group's compassion for animals also brings some of the tamer creatures to more

Bill Dow

Actress Tippi Hedren with one of many big cats at her Shambala wildlife preserve.

than 100 schools and libraries a year. Birthday parties and petting zoos can also be scheduled. (818) 951-3656.

5. SHAMBALA WILDLIFE PRESERVE
ACTON

This 80-acre, cottonwood-shaded sanctuary in rustic Soledad Canyon for big cats was founded by actress Tippi Hedren in 1972. The African lions, Siberian and Bengal tigers, cougars, leopards and even a couple of elephants feel totally at home in Shambala (meaning a refuge of peace and harmony for all beings). All but a few of the animals view tour-goers from their natural pens; a few of the trusted "pets" are permitted to mingle. Shambala is open to the public one weekend each month. Visitors end their tour at a picnic site near the property's lake. Reservations are required. (805) 268-0380.

6. LONG BEACH POLICE ACADEMY
7380 E. CARSON ST., LONG BEACH

Tucked away in a quiet corner near the vacant Long Beach Naval Hospital is the final resting place of some of the department's most beloved police dogs. Under a 70-year-old carob tree lie 12 black polished headstones with laser-etched photos of dog and handler. Each pays tribute to a small legion of K-9 heroes, including an academy mascot—a beagle named Snoopy. Embedded in the concrete borders around the tombstones are the ashes of each dog. Bondo, a 4-year-old German shepherd and the first dog buried here, died in 1982 after chasing a burglary suspect; the man hit the dog on the head with a pipe wrench. A Rottweiler named Argo was killed in a three-story fall from a roof while chasing a burglary suspect. Other true and trusting friends: Justice, Kazan, Pax, Zeus and Canto. Walk through the main gate and ask the office for directions to the graveyard.

7. MARINE MAMMAL CARE CENTER
ANGELS GATE PARK, 3601 S. GAFFEY ST., SAN PEDRO

The marine mammal hospital and convalescent center is one of six such facilities that line California's coast. The center provides treatment and care for the hundreds of sick, injured, stranded or deliberately wounded marine mammals found on Los Angeles County beaches every year. Visitors can watch as trained volunteers feed and give injections to ailing seals and sea lions before they can be returned to their natural environment. The care center is open to the public every day from 9 a.m. to 4 p.m. For information, (310) 548-5677.

8. CAT LIBRARY

222 E. HARVARD ST., GLENDALE

A special collection room at the Glendale Central Library is home to the world's largest collection of cat books and other feline-related material. This library gold mine has more than 20,000 cat books, photos, sketches, oil paintings and stat-uettes, including one cat book dating back to 1837. There are cat "stud books," cat show catalogues dating from the 1890s that breeders use for pedigree searches and books of cat fiction and cat poetry. Telephone inquiries pour into the library from around the world. Books cannot be checked out or even carried from the room for photocopying. The collection is aimed at the breeder or serious cat owner. Cat peo-ple are encouraged to call before coming to make certain the librarian will be there. (818) 548-2020.

9. GRIFFITH PARK & SOUTHERN RAILROAD

GRIFFITH PARK, 4400 CRYSTAL SPRINGS, LOS ANGELES

All aboard! Take your pooch for a fun-filled, eight-minute ride. Listen to him howl when the whistle blasts and watch his ears flap as the train chugs past pens where goats, ponies, llamas and pigs live. Southern Railroad is open 10 a.m. to 4:30 p.m. weekdays, 10 a.m. to 5:30 p.m. Saturdays and Sundays. Trains run until 4:15 p.m. Train rides are $1.75 for adults, $1.25 for children 19 months to 13 years and $1 for senior citizens. Dogs ride free. (213) 664-6788.

Griffith Park's kiddie-size train is located in Travel Town, hours and prices are about the same; (213) 662-9678. For an equestrian experience, head to the pony rides at the other end of Griffith Park, near the carousel.

10. LAUREL CANYON PARK

8260 MULHOLLAND DR., STUDIO CITY

In the Hollywood Hills, south of Mulholland Drive, urban dog lovers can let their pets romp untethered in a 3.7-acre, partially fenced-off dog area. A doggie drinking fountain is available, as are key pieces of equipment in a dog park—pooper scoopers. (When their dogs do, owners must do their duty.) Dogs can frolic freely from 7 to 10 a.m. and 3 p.m. to sundown daily.

There are other "bark parks" with growing clientele: Silver Lake Recreation Center, Long Beach Recreation Park, Marine and Joslyn parks in Santa Monica (for Santa Monica residents' dogs only), Dominguez Park in Redondo Beach and unde-veloped areas in the Angeles National Forest. Check them for hours and regulations.

Equestrian Centers

For equestrian classes or nostalgic hayrides, L.A. has an assortment of riding centers and hundreds of trails.

----

1. K.C. MALIBU STABLES
400 N. KANAN ROAD (AT WHITE CLOUD RANCH), MALIBU

Guided trail rides ranging from one hour to a full day cost $20 an hour. Riders will visit some destinations along the unbeaten path, overlooking the beach and city. The stables also provide two-hour sunset rides, full-moon rides twice each month and private lessons. (818) 879-0444.

2. STONEY POINT RIDING CENTER
10861 ANDORA AVE., CHATSWORTH

In a "Mommy and Me" class, children and parents are taught how to groom the pony or horse, how to saddle it and how to mount and dismount. Parents take their children through the course by leading the pony or horse. Children are taught ter-

Jumping barriers at the Los Angeles Equestrian Center.

Joe Vitti / Los Angeles Times

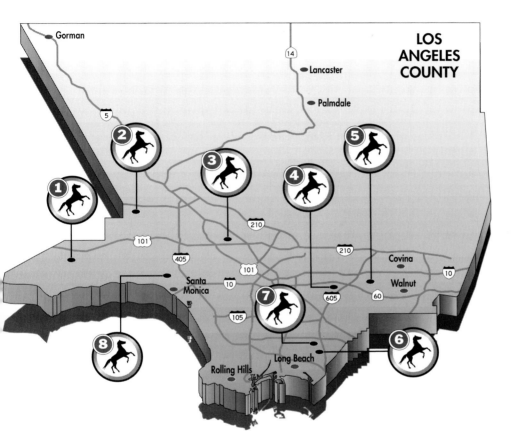

minology, and how to walk and trot on horseback. These once-a-week lessons are offered through Mason and Northridge parks and Learning Tree University. Summer lessons are geared to 4- to 7-year-olds for six weeks at $70. The center also offers clinics, workshops, trail rides, play days, boarding and holiday celebrations. Call Northridge Park (818) 349-7341 or Stoney Point Riding Center (818) 775-3839.

3. LOS ANGELES EQUESTRIAN CENTER
480 RIVERSIDE DR., BURBANK

The area in Burbank along Riverside Drive, east of the studios and west of Victory Boulevard, is home to a number of riding stables, thanks to its proximity to the trails in Griffith Park. The riding stables lack day guides but offer horse rentals for $15 an hour. A two-hour guided night ride, by reservation only, with a barbecue afterward, costs $33 per person. For reservations call (818) 840-8401 or, for equestrian events, call (818) 840-9063.

4. WHITTIER EQUESTRIAN CENTER
12191 ROOKS ROAD, WHITTIER

This 20-acre site with 35 horses and almost 300 miles of trails is in a bucolic setting near the Whittier Narrows Nature Center and Wildlife Sanctuary. During the summer, riders can travel across the shallow river and through the tall clusters of bamboo that grow in pools every winter. It is open seven days a week beginning late June. Private riding lessons and guided trail rides cost $15 per hour. (310) 699-5911.

5. INDUSTRY HILLS EQUESTRIAN CENTER
16000 TEMPLE AVE., CITY OF INDUSTRY

Reservations are required to book hayrides in the rustic area near the 300-acre equestrian center and the hills beyond, which offer panoramic views of Los Angeles, Mt. Baldy and the San Bernardino Mountains. Rides can begin or end with a catered barbecue. Hayrides are $5 per person, with a 40-person minimum. City dwellers may delight in guided one- and two-hour trail rides for $15 and $25; private lessons at $20 per half-hour; horse and livestock shows, including camel and ostrich bareback events; charity rodeos, and snail and armadillo races. (818) 854-2370.

6. LARRY'S PONY RIDES
7600 SPRING ST., LONG BEACH

Belgian draft horses pull hay wagons along the roadway of rustic El Dorado Park in Long Beach. Hayrides, along with picnics and barbecues, may be scheduled any time until midnight for 120 people. Hour-long rides are $7.50 per person with a $75 minimum; half-hour rides are $5 with a $75 minimum. Buggy rides, with a coachman in tails and top hat, are $100 an hour. Other festive options include pony rides and a petting zoo that will travel to the party site. (310) 865-3290.

7. LAKEWOOD EQUESTRIAN CENTER
11369 E. CARSON ST., LAKEWOOD

The 38-acre, country-atmosphere site with 200 horses east of the San Gabriel River, sports everything from three riding schools and seven large arenas to pony rides and a petting zoo. Boarding and training provided; private lessons cost $30 for 30 minutes and the same for one-hour group lessons. No rentals. (310) 425-1905.

8. WILL ROGERS EQUESTRIAN CENTER
1603 WILL ROGERS STATE PARK ROAD, PACIFIC PALISADES

Families can picnic while watching polo matches every weekend. It's a chance to enjoy horses and watch polo as humorist Will Rogers did here long ago. There is a $5 parking fee. At the equestrian center, a guide can take small groups on trail rides for $35 an hour, by appointment only. Private riding lessons cost $50 an hour. (310) 454-8212 or (310) 573-7270.

Jogging Paths

Some of the well-trod and scenic routes
for runners in Los Angeles County.

----

1. HESSE PARK
29201 HAWTHORNE BLVD., RANCHO PALOS VERDES

From the west edge of Hesse Park, the land drops away sharply to the Pacific Ocean. The wind off the ocean provides the best air found in Greater Los Angeles. The park features various exercise stations for stretching and warming up. One drawback is the park's relatively small size. The quarter-mile loop around the perimeter can become monotonous, but the expansive view of mountains, sea and clouds makes it worthwhile.

2. SAN VICENTE BOULEVARD
SANTA MONICA

The grassy median of San Vicente Boulevard is a four-mile run from Ocean Avenue to the Los Angeles city limits and back. The route is well known in the entertainment industry because many film and music-business types commute along the corridor between Hollywood and Pacific Palisades and Malibu. Unemployed actors, screenwriters and technical directors would do well to mix their business and cardiovascular conditioning here.

3. EXPOSITION PARK AREA
EXPOSITION BOULEVARD AND FIGUEROA STREET, LOS ANGELES

This is a popular green space used by joggers in South Los Angeles. Although this busy neighborhood is also home to the Coliseum, the Sports Arena and two large museums, a jog along the rows of old, stately trees and around the park's 7.5-acre rose garden can be an escape from the sounds of the city. Street parking is easier to find on weekends.

■ "Exposition Park's Colorful History," see Page 141.

4. SEPULVEDA BASIN RECREATION AREA
SAN FERNANDO VALLEY, NORTHWEST OF THE JUNCTION OF THE SAN DIEGO AND VENTURA FREEWAYS

The San Fernando Valley is hot. The Santa Monica Mountains cut off most of the onshore airflow. Valley joggers know that if the temperature forecast for downtown Los Angeles is 80 degrees, the Valley usually tops 90. Many runners go out in

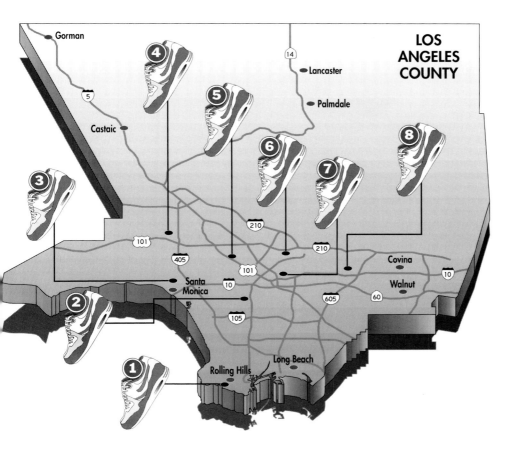

the early morning, and a favorite spot is the Sepulveda Basin, which features long pedestrian and bike routes, both paved and unpaved, running parallel to Burbank Boulevard. Curving past the cluster of golf courses, parks and wildlife areas, the paths are a nice change of pace from the old neighborhood loop.

5. HOLLYWOOD RESERVOIR
HOLLYWOOD HILLS, OFF BARHAM BOULEVARD

Behind 188-foot-high Mulholland Dam lies Hollywood Reservoir, encircled by pine and sycamore-covered slopes. The facility, completed in 1924, is operated by the Department of Water and Power. Use of the 3.2-mile asphalt path along the lake's perimeter brings out the poetry in some joggers. They speak of "an other-worldly atmosphere" and "Zen-like tranquillity." Open to public from 6:30 to 10 a.m. and 2 to 6:30 p.m. daily, and 6:30 a.m. to 6:30 p.m. weekends. No dogs allowed.

Walkers, bikers and a jogger share West Drive in the Arroyo Seco.

Mike Meadows / Los Angeles Times

6. ARROYO SECO
PASADENA

Pasadena's Arroyo Seco offers many options for runners. Lower Arroyo Park (enter from the 300 block of South Arroyo Boulevard) is about a mile south of the Rose Bowl. The right-of-way belongs to joggers, walkers (dogs must be on leashes) and equestrians. From sunset to sunrise the traffic consists mostly of coyotes, skunks and raccoons. Another popular location is the loop around the Rose Bowl and Brookside Golf Course—about three miles. Unless there is a sporting event or flea market in progress at the Rose Bowl, there is usually plenty of parking.

7. CAL STATE L.A.
5151 STATE UNIVERSITY DR., LOS ANGELES

The Cal State L.A. campus is near the intersection of the San Bernardino and Long Beach freeways, high on a hill. The elevation provides a steady breeze. The eight-lane track at the athletic field is composed of a slightly spongy synthetic material that resembles reddish-orange cottage cheese. It is easier on the feet than pavement. Cal State L.A. is convenient to most of East Los Angeles. Parking meters charge 25 cents an hour. The track is open from 6 a.m. to dusk.

8. WHITTIER NARROWS RECREATION AREA
823 LEXINGTON-GALLATIN ROAD, SOUTH EL MONTE

There is nothing in the San Gabriel Valley quite like Whittier Narrows. It is county land straddling the junction of Rosemead Boulevard and the Pomona Freeway. Including undeveloped areas, this sprawling matrix of softball fields, picnic areas, tree-strewn parkland, interconnecting man-made lakes and wildlife sanctuary covers 1.7 square miles (1,092 acres). Runners can go for miles on dirt roads and paths without backtracking.

Exposition Park's Colorful History

Before the turn of the century, Agricultural Park filled the site now occupied by Exposition Park's celebrated rose garden. There, folks could watch horse, camel, dog, bicycle and auto races, get a drink at the city's longest bar and—if they were so inclined—repair to one of the city's more stylish brothels.

On Sept. 10, 1906, Agricultural Park was the scene of a real demolition derby. Before a cheering crowd of 25,000, two steam locomotives began huffing and puffing, building up steam for a head-on collision. Promoters had a mile of track laid for the staged event. Ads were placed weeks in advance in all the papers and 200 police officers were hired for crowd control.

The two engineers jumped to safety only seconds before the engines crashed at 50 m.p.h. After the dust settled, the crowd began collecting souvenirs from the wreckage and the promoters complained about losing $7,000 on the event.

William Miller Bowen, a sharp-eyed attorney and devout Methodist, embarked on a marathon lawsuit—at his own expense—to make Agricultural Park public property. He succeeded in 1908 and went to work to convert the site to more sedate, albeit less colorful, recreation.

The saloons and brothel that once brought gamblers and a seedy clientele to the park were torn down in 1910. Long-awaited plans were finally laid out for the National Guard armory, an exposition building (now the Museum of Science and Industry), the Museum of Natural History and, later, a seven-acre sunken rose garden with 15,000 rosebushes.

The park's opening ceremonies in November, 1913, included breaking a bottle

Pyramid-like towers stood at the main entrance to Agricultural Park on Wesley Avenue.

Security Pacific Collection

141

Formal opening of Exposition Park in 1913.

of Owens River water from the new aqueduct on the cornerstone of the National Guard armory.

Today you can't get a drink or place a bet in Exposition Park anymore, but you can stop and smell those roses.

L.A.'s Stairways

Forget traffic and parking hassles. Get off the freeway, enjoy the cardiovascular benefits of these historic steps.

1. HOLLYWOODLAND
2795 WOODSHIRE DR. TO 2872 BELDEN DR.

At the foot of the Hollywood sign, which was erected in 1923 to advertise the Hollywoodland subdivision, visitors and residents climb the six tucked-away stairways in the cozy community of Beachwood Canyon. From the shaded granite steps, climbers get glimpses of terraced cactus gardens, morning glories, fig trees and vistas of canyon homes. More than 124 steps between Woodshire and Belden drives await the urban hiker. Other stairways can be found between the 2800 and 3000 blocks of Beachwood Drive.

These stairs in Silver Lake were featured in a 1932 Laurel and Hardy film.

Axel Koester / Los Angeles Times

2. 'MUSIC BOX' STAIRWAY
900 BLOCK VENDOME STREET, SILVER LAKE

One of the cinema's most famous staircases was used in the 1932 Academy Award-winning short film "The Music Box," in which Laurel and Hardy portray bumbling piano delivery men. The vacant lot that was next to the stairway in the movie is now filled with buildings, but a commemorative plaque at the foot of the steps makes it unmistakable. Modern lamps and a metal handrail have been installed, but many of the surrounding houses remain unchanged.

Near Earl Street and Bancroft Avenue are the gigantic zigzagging Earl Street steps, which, like many in the neighborhood, were built as shortcuts to streetcar lines.

Rising from the Silver Lake

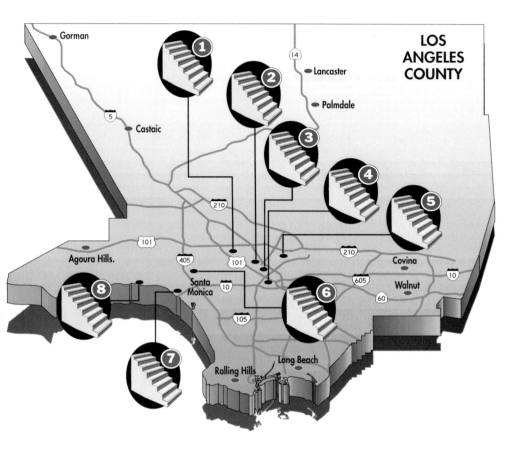

reservoir to Apex Avenue are the Cove Avenue steps, offering a dizzying view of the water and hills. From here, climbers connect with the nearby Loma Vista Place steps and the Ayr Street steps. Along the Ayr steps are small bungalows called "step houses" that are reachable only by steps.

3. L.A.'S LONGEST STAIRWAY
BAXTER PLACE AND AVON STREET, ELYSIAN HEIGHTS

In this nearly hidden canyon northeast of Elysian Park is a lofty, steep concrete stairway about a quarter-block from the intersection. Its 230 steps, at places overgrown with vegetation, are believed to make up the longest stairway in Los Angeles. As it zigzags up, climbers pass a grassy hillside spotted with jade plant and ice plant. At the top, a reward of breathtaking views of the Hollywood sign and Griffith Observatory is yours.

4. BUNKER HILL STEPS
BETWEEN 4TH AND 5TH STREETS, WEST OF GRAND AVENUE

In the heart of Downtown, the sound of a cascading waterfall soothes the nerves on Bunker Hill along 103 steps known locally as Cardiac Hill. This five-story climb, built in imitation of the Spanish Steps in Rome, links the new L.A. on the hill to the old Los Angeles along 5th Street. The city's newest and grandest public stairway, built at a cost of $12 million, is scented with cafe au lait and terraced with bistros. Some who are not so energetic navigate labyrinthine routes just to avoid it.

5. GRIMKE STAIRWAY
GRIMKE WAY NEAR YORK BOULEVARD AND FIGUEROA STREET, HIGHLAND PARK

Explore this small, charming hillside neighborhood of Mt. Angelus, with its lush gardens and well-maintained homes. This quiet refuge of shady streets and houses from different eras and architectural styles looks like a layer cake put together by six bakers. It is traversed by nine city-owned staircases, pedestrian-only thoroughfares that were built more than 70 years ago as alternatives to the winding roads. Here the stairways tunnel through a profusion of wild vegetation. Beware: stairway gates are sometimes locked.

6. JANSS STAIRWAY
SUNSET BOULEVARD AND HILGARD AVENUE, WEST LOS ANGELES

When Edwin and Harold Janss, the developers of Westwood Village, bestowed a $50,000 gift on UCLA in 1930, the brothers had in mind the building of a gateway from their village to the university. UCLA instead opted to gussy up its eastern flank with a 195-foot-long, 18-foot-wide, red-brick stairway that rises gracefully from the gymnasiums to Royce and Murphy halls. The Janss Steps have since racked up quite a bit of history. JFK, Adlai Stevenson and Martin Luther King Jr. gave speeches there. The stairs provide a tough workout for dedicated walkers and joggers.

7. ULTIMATE STAIRWAY
300 BLOCK ADELAIDE DRIVE, SANTA MONICA

The E-ticket Stairmaster of nearly 200 steps brings exercise devotees in droves to this idyllic spot. So, too, do its ocean view, abundance of greenery and a breeze on hot days. These outdoor steps, with a grassy expanse that divides 4th Street at the north end, plunge down Santa Monica Canyon to the intersection of Entrada Drive and Ocean Avenue. Local TV news shows and magazines have portrayed the steps as the hippest thing to happen to exercise since Spandex. Some of the unwritten rules of step etiquette here are: no perfume or spitting (they provoke nausea), no clanging bracelets, let faster steppers pass by, no fooling with people's makeshift counters (rocks and leaves that fitness fanatics use to keep track of repetitions). So dedicated are these stair folk that when an ambulance once came to fetch a fallen runner, they kept running past the paramedic team until firefighters had to close down the stairway.

About a dozen other, less-crowded public staircases and walkways are found in Santa Monica Canyon, including a brick-lined one about 100 feet west of the 4th Street stairway.

8. CASTELLAMMARE STAIRWAYS

SUNSET BOULEVARD AND CASTELLAMMARE DRIVE,
PACIFIC PALISADES

Castellammare, a steep hillside enclave of million-dollar homes, was named for a region in Sicily. It is noted for its mudslides, dead-end stairways and the former home of actress and comedienne Thelma Todd, known as the "Vamping Venus," whose death here in 1935 has been linked by some authors to the Mob.

There are seven public stairways in Pacific Palisades, including a 1927 concrete stairway off Posetano Road near Castellammare that ascends to Revello Drive, and another where Breve Way joins Porto Marina Way.

Note: Other areas with picturesque stairs include Los Feliz, Mt. Washington, Franklin Heights, Whitley Heights and El Sereno.

Source: "Stairway Walks in Los Angeles" by Adah Bakalinsky and Larry Gordon and published by Wilderness Press in Berkeley.

Hearts, Flowers and More

Some offbeat ways to romance that special someone on Valentine's Day.

----

1. DON'S EARLY LIGHT
42741 N. 45TH ST. WEST, UNIT G, QUARTZ HILL

High-altitude types can be uplifted on a sunrise hot-air balloon ride above the Antelope Valley, complete with champagne during and after the flight. Post-flight breakfasts at a nearby restaurant are included with the flights, which range from $70 to $125 per person. (800) 943-7616.

2. RED BARON AIR ADS
12653 OSBORNE ST., PACOIMA

When only a grand gesture will do, consider calling the Red Baron. Your tender message of love (tender but succinct—the limit is 40 characters) will be set in five- or seven-foot-high red block letters and towed on a banner across the skies of Los Angeles, circling above your sweetheart's home or workplace. The average one-hour cost is $250. (818) 896-6667.

3. SUNSET RANCH STABLES
3400 N. BEACHWOOD DR., LOS ANGELES

Saddle up for a moonlight trail ride through Griffith Park, into Burbank and to a sprawling hacienda, where riders head in for a leisurely candlelight dinner. The ride alone is three hours. Friday night price is $35 per person (not including dinner). Other nights of the week are reserved for private groups of 15 or more. (213) 464-9612 or (213) 469-5450.

4. SHAKESPEARE BRIDGE
FRANKLIN AVENUE BETWEEN MYRA AVENUE AND ST. GEORGE STREET, LOS FELIZ

It may not be the Golden Gate, but use your imagination. Take a late-night drive or stroll over this beloved 1925 landmark, which, with its Gothic turrets and arches, remains one of the city's most photographed and most whimsical spans.

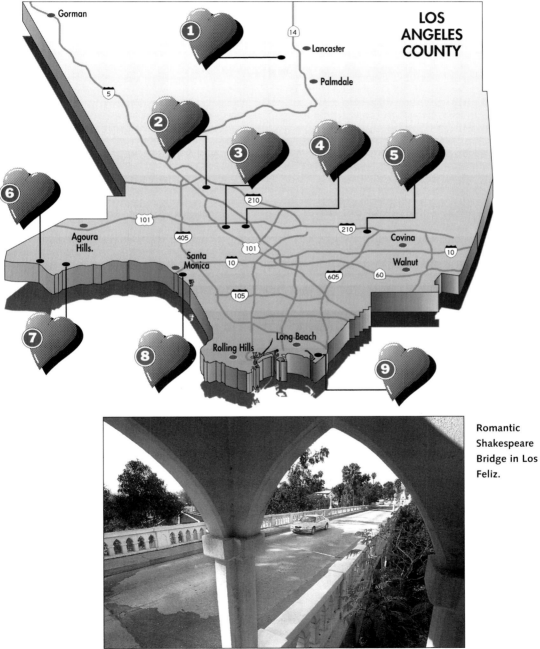

LOS
ANGELES
COUNTY

Gorman

1

14

Lancaster

Palmdale

2

3

4

5

6

5

101

Agoura
Hills.

405

Santa
Monica

101

10

210

210

Covina

Walnut

10

60

605

105

7

8

Rolling Hills

Long Beach

9

Romantic
Shakespeare
Bridge in Los
Feliz.

Ken Hively / Los Angeles Times

149

5. BARTON HORSE-DRAWN CARRIAGES
ARCADIA

If that clip-clop horse-and-carriage sound gets you all mushy and nostalgic, take a romantic drive in a vehicle just right for you. Turn back the clock and take a carriage ride to a leisurely picnic in a secluded meadow. For 27 years the Barton family has trailered a horse and one of its 20-plus vintage carriages anywhere in Southern California, to take you in style to dinner, to the park or just around the block to impress the neighbors. Drivers dress in top hats and red livery. Fees begin at $500 and are based on how far the equipment travels. (818) 447-6693.

6. EL PESCADOR, EL MATADOR AND LA PIEDRA STATE BEACHES
32000 BLOCK PACIFIC COAST HIGHWAY, MALIBU

A trio of beaches, nestled beneath the bluffs along Pacific Coast Highway—part of the Robert Meyer Memorial State Beach—is tailor-made for daylight or evening romantic strolls, with rarely more than a few people dotting the sand. Why not take along some gourmet fantasies in a lavish picnic basket?

7. MALIBU SUNSET

For superlatively awesome sunsets, drive north on Pacific Coast Highway into Malibu. Turn right on Corral Canyon Road and then drive to the top, where the road ends. Walk the trail off to the right. From atop some boulders, there is an idyllic view of the ocean, the mountains and even the San Fernando Valley.

8. SANTA MONICA AIR TOURS
2907 6TH ST., SUITE 100, SANTA MONICA

Here's something for everyone who needs to get a relationship off the ground. "Mile-High Adventures" offers couples a one-hour moonlight flight aboard a twin-engine plane equipped with romantic amenities that include a "cloud-like featherbed" in a cabin "securely partitioned off from the cockpit." When the plane reaches 5,286 feet, the pilot rocks the wings "to let the couple know they have reached that 'golden' altitude." Basic cost is $285 to $329; options include round-trip limousine service and a three-course gourmet dinner. (310) 450-4447.

9. GONDOLA GETAWAYS
5437 E. OCEAN BLVD., LONG BEACH

For an hour of waterborne smooching, a gondolier (who may even sing to you) will propel you around the canals and waterways of Naples Island at Belmont Shore, while you munch on French bread, cheese and salami, which they provide, and listen to Italian music. Bring the beverage of your choice; they provide the ice and glasses. Costs $55 per couple. (310) 433-9595.

Fourth of July Celebrations

Angelenos can find a dazzling array of Independence Day revelry, ranging from the patriotic to the zany.

----

1. PIERCE COLLEGE
6201 WINNETKA AVE., WOODLAND HILLS

The annual Fourth of July show begins at 5:30 p.m. with a pre-fireworks show, including musical acts, bands, dancers and sky-diving. Advance tickets are $9 for adults and $7 for senior citizens and children 12 and under. Parking is $5. For ticket information, call (818) 703-7859.

2. CASTAIC LAKE
32132 RIDGE ROUTE ROAD, CASTAIC

A combination of fireworks, music and marching bands headlines the pyro-musical "Spirit of America" celebrations at the Castaic Lake Recreation Area. Part of the proceeds goes to the Castaic Middle School library. Advance tickets are $15 per car or van; $20 at the gate. No walk-ins. Gates open at 5:30 p.m. For more information, call (805) 257-4050.

The Hollywood Bowl's annual extravaganza follows a celebration of traditional American music from the Los Angeles Philharmonic.

3. HOLLYWOOD BOWL
2301 N. HIGHLAND AVE., HOLLYWOOD

The Los Angeles Philharmonic begins the traditional musical celebration with "America the Beautiful." A grand finale of fireworks display by Pyro-Spectaculars coordinates with uncanny precision to the beats of John Philip Sousa marches. Show begins at 7:30. Reservations required, prices vary. (213) 850-2000.

■ **"The Old Rugged Cross of Cahuenga Pass," see Page 155.**

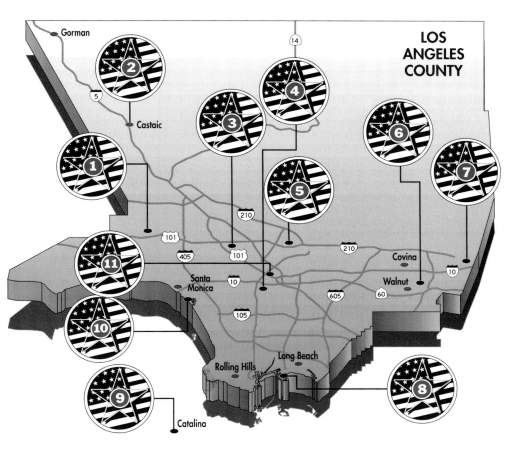

4. BARNES PARK
350 S. MCPHERRIN AVE., MONTEREY PARK

Independence Day celebrations at Barnes Memorial Park have included Monterey Park residents becoming U.S. citizens. Other traditional festivities: pie-eating contests, a water balloon toss, sack races, a horseshoe contest, hayrides, live music and fireworks. Celebrations begin at 1 p.m. Free.

5. ROSE BOWL
1001 ROSE BOWL DR., PASADENA

The annual, lavish fireworks show begins at 7 p.m., with gates opening at 5:30 p.m. Tickets start at $9 for adults and $7 for children and are available through the Rose Bowl box office or Ticketmaster outlets. The grassy area around the stadium will also be open to the public for free aerial sky concert viewing, but parking will cost $5. For more information, call (800) 963-4600.

6. ROWLAND HIGH SCHOOL
2000 S. OTTERBEIN AVE., WALNUT

Rowland Heights sponsors a family evening of fun and fireworks on the high school football field. The show would not be complete without a performance by the Rowland Heights High School Band. Festivities begin at 8 p.m. (818) 965-3448.

Mt. San Antonio College's annual Fourth of July Fireworks Show has always been the product of several area communities. Entertainment in the past includes sky-divers, cavalry troops, food booths, band competitions, live music, fireworks and canine Frisbee acrobatics. This event has been cancelled in the past, please call before attending. (909) 595-6138.

7. FAIRPLEX
1101 W. MCKINLEY AVE., POMONA

In addition to fireworks, annual Kaboom Celebrations have featured pig races, carnival rides, a dunking tank, a petting farm, food booths, musical entertainment, a classic car show and a chili cook-off. The event starts at 3 p.m. Tickets are $5 for adults and $3 for children 6 to 12. Parking is $4 at Gate 17. For information, call (909) 623-3111.

8. QUEEN MARY
1126 QUEENS HIGHWAY, PIER J, LONG BEACH

Go aboard the Queen Mary and watch the fireworks explode over Long Beach Harbor, or watch free from the shore. A 30-minute fireworks show begins at 9 p.m. Parking is $10 in the Queen Mary lot. General admission is $10, admission for children 4 to 11 is $6 and children under 4 are free. Call (310) 435-3511.

The Long Beach Fire Department's annual fireworks display takes place at Long Beach Veterans Stadium, 500 Lew Davis Dr. Adults $6, senior citizens and children 5 to 11, $5. Show starts at 5:30 p.m.

9. AVALON BAY
SANTA CATALINA ISLAND

Islanders kick off the celebration with dinghy races at Two Harbors and an old-fashioned parade on Crescent Avenue featuring the Marine Corps Band. The parade begins at 1 p.m. Free. Visitors may take part in a Fourth of July dinner dance at the historic Casino Ballroom, from which they can view the fireworks display. Reservations required. Call (310) 510-1520.

10. VENICE BEACH RECREATION CENTER
1800 OCEAN FRONT WALK, VENICE BEACH

Venice Beach holds its annual muscle contest, featuring couples moving and posing to music at 2 p.m. Registration fee. Spectators free. (310) 399-2775.

11. DODGER STADIUM
1000 ELYSIAN PARK AVE., LOS ANGELES

Postgame exploding fireworks light up Dodger Stadium as multicolor glaring rockets snap, crackle and burst through the sky. Every year the extravaganza ignites a sellout crowd and a percussion band booms and clangs a musical overture.

■ "How the Dodgers Got Their Home," see Page 157.

Other communities that usually offer authorized fireworks displays are: Agua Dulce, Alhambra, Artesia, Baldwin Park, Bell Gardens, Burbank, Cerritos, Claremont, Downey, El Segundo, Gardena, Glendora, Huntington Park, Inglewood, Irwindale, La Crescenta, Lancaster, La Verne, Lawndale, Los Angeles, Lynwood, Marina del Rey, Maywood, Montebello, Palmdale, Rosemead, Santa Fe Springs, Saugus, South Gate, South Pasadena, Torrance, Valencia and West Covina.

Note: Not all of Los Angeles County's 88 cities still permit "safe and sane" fireworks. For information about other fireworks celebrations and questions about fireworks in your area, call the county Fire Department at (800) 900-3473.

The Old Rugged Cross of Cahuenga Pass

For more than 70 years, a 34-foot illuminated cross looming over the Cahuenga Pass has been one of the landmarks by which motorists mark their passage between downtown and the San Fernando Valley.

The cross was a memorial to one of Hollywood's pioneers, Christine Wetherell Stevenson, the heiress to the Pittsburgh Paint fortune who helped arrange construction of the Hollywood Bowl. An aspiring playwright, she wrote "The Pilgrimage Play," a pageant about the life and teachings of Jesus Christ.

In 1920 Stevenson chose 29 acres across the Cahuenga Pass from the Hollywood Bowl and helped carry stones from the nearby hills to build the open-air Pilgrimage Theater. She died two years later and in 1923 her admirers planted the cross on the hill above the theater in her memory.

Within six years a brush fire destroyed the original theater, and in 1931 Stevenson's drama reopened in a concrete theater designed in an "ancient Judaic style."

For many years the cross was lighted only at Easter and during the annual "Pilgrimage Play" season. But the public's affection for the landmark grew, and soon Sunday school children were donating money to keep the cross lit. Ultimately, Southern California Edison Co. assumed that expense and bore it until 1941, when the theater and cross were donated to the county.

After the county supervisors accepted the gift, they renamed the theater after Supervisor John Anson Ford, recognizing his 24 years of service to the district in which the theater is located. The play continued its

Cross above freeway today.

Luis Sinco / Los Angeles Times

The Pilgrimage Theater in 1926. The Cahuenga Pass facility was destroyed in a 1929 brush fire, rebuilt in 1931 and renamed the John Anson Ford Theater in 1941 after it was donated to Los Angeles County.

Los Angeles Times

annual run until 1964, when the first in a series of lawsuits triggered by the facility's religious uses forced an end to the performances.

The cross was damaged by fire a year later. The county replaced it with a steel and plexiglass structure and operated it routinely for years. But the tradition came under legal fire in 1978, when a California Supreme Court ruling ended Los Angeles' 30-year practice of lighting City Hall windows to form a cross at Christmas and Easter. Two years later, a college professor successfully argued in court that the county was violating the constitutional separation of church and state by maintaining the Ford theater cross as well.

The cross, however, remained—dark and unguarded, abused and unused. Vandals chipped away at its foundation until a windstorm knocked it over it 1984.

Afterward, a small group of crusaders began raising funds for a new cross by doing a video documentary, recording a song, "The Ballad of the Hollywood Cross" by Mindas Masiulis, and collaborating with the Hollywood Heritage preservation group.

Almost 10 years later, with little fanfare, a new cross was erected on the small hilltop patch after the group purchased the site from the county.

The glowing landmark rising above the Cahuenga Pass had survived wind and rain and, finally, even a strict construction of the Constitution.

How the Dodgers Got Their Home

In the years of hope and expansion in the 1950s, Los Angeles was a city that seemed to have all the ingredients for greatness, except for one thing—a major league baseball team.

The Music Center was on the drawing boards, the great thoroughfare of Interstate 10 was being built, and the bustling plants of Lockheed and McDonnell Douglas were cranking out the latest aircraft, drawing thousands in search of work.

But for all the signs of growth, when it came to baseball, L.A. was still in the minor leagues—the only baseball in town was played by the triple-A Hollywood Stars and the Los Angeles Angels.

When rumors surfaced that Brooklyn Dodger owner Walter O'Malley might be interested in moving his team to Los Angeles, city fathers leaped at the chance.

O'Malley was disgruntled with the dilapidated shape of his team's ballpark, Ebbets Field. New York City had offered him a chance to move to Flushing Meadows. But O'Malley was enticed by an offer from Los Angeles officials, who promised to build him a stadium of grand proportions using county retirement funds. In the meantime, they offered him use of the Coliseum.

O'Malley finally decided to pull up stakes and move west in 1957. Plus, he persuaded New York Giants owner Horace Stoneham to move his team to San Francisco so at least some games could be played on the West Coast without a cross-country trip.

Many New York fans have branded them traitors ever since.

For four seasons, the Dodgers played in the Coliseum while O'Malley dreamed of having his own stadium—built his own way and exactly where he wanted it.

A few years earlier, while visiting L.A., O'Malley had seen a patch of eroded gul-

The future site of Dodger Stadium, shown from the air in 1960.

Pacific Air Industries

Chavez Ravine was once a rural area with unpaved streets.

Marsha T. Goorman / Los Angeles Times

lies, stunted trees and a few ramshackle dwellings. The site, known as Chavez Ravine, had been turned down by Disney as a possible location for its amusement park.

But O'Malley liked the site. It was only two miles from downtown and accessible by every major highway in the Los Angeles area.

But he couldn't have picked a more controversial location. It had formerly housed a close-knit community of at least 1,000 Mexican Americans who called the rugged hills of Chavez Ravine home. To them, it was called Palo Verde, or Green Tree.

It was rural, with unpaved roads, back-yard farms, and goats, sheep and cattle roaming the terrain. Palo Verde was an area where children would take wooden carts, fit them with wheelbarrow wheels and ride fast down the hills.

By the time O'Malley arrived, most residents had been evicted to make way for a federally funded housing project. The city, however, refused to have anything to do with the project, and the site had remained vacant for several years.

Finally, the federal government agreed to sell the land to the city for $1.3 million—a $4-million loss—with the condition that it be used "for public purposes only."

In 1958 the city agreed to trade the land in Chavez Ravine for nine acres that O'Malley owned at Avalon Boulevard and 42nd Place, the site of Wrigley Field.

O'Malley was now set to begin construction of Dodger Stadium. But more problems were still ahead.

About 20 residents in the area refused to accept the city's buyout offer and remained in their cluster of modest homes.

On May 9, 1959, the city moved to evict them. Television cameras recorded one particularly ugly confrontation with the Arechiga family, who had lived there 36 years.

Four sheriff's deputies carried one daughter, kicking and screaming, out of the house and arrested her for battery; her mother, Abrana, cursed at everyone. Chickens, dogs and a turkey ran wildly as bulldozers pulled down the house. The head of the family, Manuel Arechiga, set up a tent and refused to budge, saying he had no place to go.

Public sympathy was aroused. A trailer company provided to the Arechigas the latest and most expensive model available.

Several days later, the Los Angeles Mirror reported that the Arechiga family as a whole owned 11 dwellings in the city and therefore did have a place to go.

The Arechigas accepted the city's offer of $10,500.

The families were all removed, and O'Malley began building his $20-million stadium on Sept. 17, 1959.

Dodger Stadium officially opened on April 10, 1962. O'Malley, ever the businessman, allowed only two drinking fountains—one in each team's dugout—to help boost refreshment sales.

The next season, the Dodgers beat the New York Yankees in the World Series. Factory sirens blared, horns honked, strangers clapped each other on the back. Chavez Ravine had now become a gathering place for the new Los Angeles, with the community that once occupied the site becoming a part of the city's history.

Halloween Haunts

Across L.A. County, Halloween spirits come alive with haunted houses, horror stagings and visual delights.

----

1. SPOOKY HOUSE
VANOWEN AND VARIEL STREETS, WOODLAND HILLS

Spooks and goblins invade the Valley Indoor Swapmeet, where Bob Koritzke, Dave Rector and brave Woodland Hills Youth Club spirits amaze guests on a terror tour of a specially engineered torture chamber. Refreshments and parking are available. For one hour each day, beginning at twilight, the show is toned down for younger spirits. Admission $5.50. (818) 888-8570.

2. BURIED ALIVE
16017 DEVONSHIRE ST., GRANADA HILLS

Lucifer's grave ignites in flames when anyone approaches at Gary Farajian and Dave Cash's annual earthly haunt. The two friends have excavated most of Farajian's yard, digging two waist-deep graves and an underground tunnel system. On Halloween night, the two hosts are alternately "killed" and thrown into the grave, only to escape through the tunnel and sneak up behind an unsuspecting audience. The

Gary Farajian guards his graveyard on Devonshire Street in Granada Hills.

Lori Shepler / Los Angeles Times

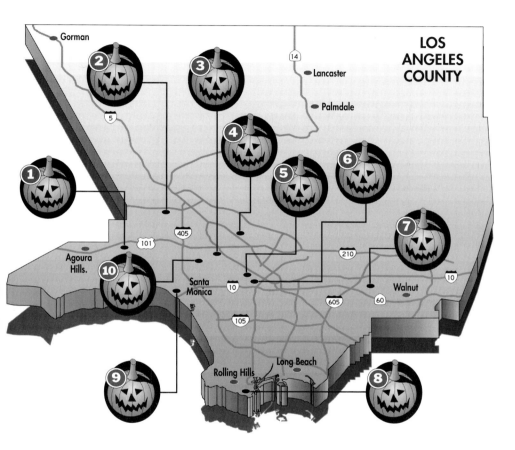

other side of the yard sports a guillotine, hangman's post and headsman's ax. The executioner's gory handiwork is strewn about. Free.

3. HALLOWED HAUNTING GROUNDS
4343 BABCOCK AVE., STUDIO CITY

A sophisticated sound system with 40 speaker channels and trick projection techniques helps set the atmosphere in the graveyard of the desolate spirits, whose torment is expressed in the sounds of dry winds and bleating voices. Conveyors whisk spirits around the headstones, while a ghostly harpist and organist assist in hosting Gary Corb's annual event. Shows are continuous from 7 p.m. to midnight. Free.

4. DOUBLE TROUBLE GRAVEYARD
513 AND 529 N. FLORENCE ST., BURBANK

Take a stroll through the annual haunts of Keith La Prath and his partner in horror, Dick Norton. The two yards feature mummies, zombies and a scarecrow. In the cemetery, a hand emerges from a grave and what happens then to the gravedigger is worse than death—but not as bad as what happens to those who sit in the electric chair. Free.

Other free residential haunts in Burbank: 1219 N. Myers St., 806 E. Olive Ave., 3500 View Crest Dr., 2440 N. Orchard Dr., 1817 N. Pepper St., 3322 Brace Canyon Road, 1321 and 1420 Morningside Dr. and 1808 Chandler Blvd.

5. LAPD HAUNTED HOUSE
2710 W. TEMPLE ST., LOS ANGELES

The Rampart Division of the Los Angeles Police Department is among the busiest and roughest in the city, but the station's annual haunted house offers a dash of small-town fun for families. Open 6 to 10 p.m. Free.

The Wilshire Division, at 4861 Venice Blvd., also hosts a free haunted house and carnival for neighborhood children from 6 to 9 p.m. on Halloween.

6. HUTCHINSON-BUTLER FAMILY HAUNT
1500 4TH AVE., LOS ANGELES

At Joann Hutchinson-Butler's scary holiday haunt, spiders are perched in sticky cobwebs, a corpse sits bolt-upright in a coffin and mourners walk around the horrifying graveyard to the shrieking delight of neighborhood children. Black lights and background music lure horror-seekers of all ages. Free.

7. DELHAVEN COMMUNITY CENTER
15135 FAIRGROVE AVE., LA PUENTE

Halloween revelers with a taste for terror can get their fill as they journey through the Haunted Graveyard, Jungle of Terror, Crazy Man's Cove, Bloodsucker's Barnyard and Horror House Tunnels. There are also a carnival, fortunetelling, movies and a room with touch-and-feel "innards" from 6 to 8 p.m. Admission $1.

8. CHAMBER OF HORROR
10TH AND BEACON STREETS, SAN PEDRO

The Beacon House men's alcohol and drug recovery program sponsors a haunted house in the center's Victorian home, built in 1896. Every Halloween, residents of the nonprofit recovery program transform the rooms into mazes and halls of horror. The scary fun begins with refreshments and treats at 6 p.m. Admission is $1 for adults and 25 cents for children.

9. THEATER OF VAMPIRES
1238 LINCOLN BLVD., SANTA MONICA

The Santa Monica Jaycees transform the Boys and Girls Club of Santa Monica into a theater of vampires. The doors to terror will open for the less squeamish from 7 to 10 p.m., and a show tailored to the more easily frightened crowd will be offered from noon to 3 p.m. Admission $2. (310) 393-9629.

The Witch's
Cottage in
Beverly Hills.

Alan J. Duignan / Los Angeles Times

10. THE WITCH'S COTTAGE
WALDEN DRIVE AND CARMELITA AVENUE, BEVERLY HILLS

In the middle of Beverly Hills, without shrubbery or walls to hide a view, sits the fairy-tale home of the witch who tried to eat Hansel and Gretel. The year-round spirit of Halloween lingers in this 3,800-square-foot house with its steep, gabled roof and lawn bisected by a moat. It was built by set designer Henry Oliver in 1921 as a film production office in Culver City and was later moved to become a residence in Beverly Hills. Drive or stroll by this visual delight.

Christmas Lights

Here is a sampling of Los Angeles' best-dressed neighborhoods and spectacular light displays.

----

1. WOODLAND HILLS
OAKDALE AVENUE

Candy Cane Lane, a four-block neighborhood of ranch-style homes, is tucked away like a magical world, lighting up the community as it has for almost half a century. Its dazzling salutes using yuletide ornaments can be found within the boundaries of Oxnard Street, Corbin and Winnetka avenues and the Ventura Freeway.

2. BURBANK
513 N. FLORENCE ST.

Every year for almost a quarter-century, Dick Norton—a frequent winner in Burbank's annual holiday outdoor decorating contest—takes three weeks to assemble his array of snowmen, trains, Ferris wheel with dolls, teddy bears on flying swings and merry-go-round. But his neighbors haven't given up on trying to outdo him. Other winners are at 325 N. San Fernando Blvd., 529 and 1119 N. Florence St., 730 Clybourn Ave., 2009 W. Chandler Blvd., 721 E. Grinnell Dr., 1421 N. Naomi St., 454 S. Lamer St., 914 E. Magnolia Blvd., 2001 Richard St., 3500 Viewcrest Dr., 2901 Mystic View Place and 2931 Olney Place.

For a list of addresses in Burbank's annual Holiday Outdoor Decorating Contest, contact Burbank Civic Pride at (818) 238-5560.

3. EAGLE ROCK
4364 YORK BLVD.

For more than 30 years, the Meltons, now in their 70s, have kept the holiday magic alive in their front yard with thousands of lights, Santa riding an old-fashioned bike with a big front wheel, a 10-foot angel and a Nativity scene. (Mr. Melton plays Santa.) Several viewers have offered to pay the electric bill so the Meltons won't have to turn the lights off at 10 p.m., but the couple declined.

4. LA CANADA FLINTRIDGE
4951 INDIANOLA WAY

Every Christmas for the past few years, teen-age Robert Illian has plugged in thousands of lights, a 15-foot Ferris wheel, a gondola that transports stuffed animals to the roof and back, a hot-air balloon and a sleigh that teeters on the edge of the

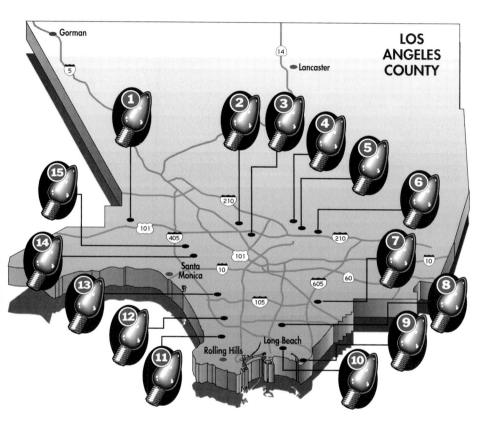

Gorman

Lancaster

Santa
Monica

Long Beach

Rolling Hills

roof. Meanwhile, his parents stand by, watching their electric meter spin. Robert constructed everything himself, including the fake snow couple, the cutout ice skaters, the gondola and the seesaw.

1418 DESCANSO DR.

It's a magical Christmas at the Descanso Gardens Festival of Lights. Thousands of lights adorn the five-acre display. Costumed actors perform Christmas tales in the Educational Pavilion. The light show continues from 6:30 to 8:30 p.m. through Dec. 30, except Sundays and evenings with wind or rain. Admission is $3 for adults, $1 for children 12 and under or free if they bring a flashlight to be part of the show.

5. ALTADENA

1960 MENDOCINO LANE

Like a community castle, the 1922 Mediterranean-style mansion owned by ice

Decorations at a home in La Canada Flintridge were constructed by teen-age Robert Illian.

Robert Durell / Los Angeles Times

cream magnate George Balian sits majestically aglow with thousands of lights at the fork of Mendocino Lane and Glenview Terrace during the holidays. Lights stay on through Jan. 1.

CHRISTMAS TREE LANE

Thousands of visitors' cars—with their headlights off—drive through what looks like an electrically enchanted forest of 111-year-old cedars, towering 100 feet high along a one-mile stretch of Santa Rosa Avenue between Woodbury Road and Altadena Drive.

6. PASADENA
UPPER HASTINGS RANCH

For almost 40 years, residents have put together showy displays to adorn their houses and yards, competing for prizes awarded by the neighborhood association. More than 1,100 homes in a 44-block area north of Sierra Madre Boulevard and west of Michillinda Avenue participate.

7. LA MIRADA
14371 RAMO DR.

Over the years, Tom and Chris Wilkinson's front yard has become a mecca for ornament lovers looking to be dazzled with dozens of decorated Christmas trees, two train sets, life-sized fabricated reindeer, sheets of ersatz snow, a miniature ski slope, a Nativity scene and nearly 15,000 lights dangling from almost everything in sight. Onlookers are urged to donate to the Wilkinsons' favorite charity, the National Center for Missing and Exploited Children.

8. CERRITOS
CASTLE PLACE AND KINGS ROW AVENUE

The Patterson and Kamppila homes are among the 30 households on this cul-de-sac caught up in a decorating frenzy. Between them, the two houses have a life-sized Teen-age Mutant Ninja Turtle in a rooftop sleigh, Nativity scenes, lights, reindeer and angels. Even the trees that line the street are wrapped with aluminum foil and spirals of plastic ribbon.

9. NAPLES
BAY SHORE WALK

In Long Beach, waterfront homes are elaborately decorated on one side and Christmas trees formed by strands of lights shimmer from water-borne platforms on the other side.

10. LONG BEACH
DAISY AVENUE

Christmas Tree Lane, a four-block stretch between 20th Street and Pacific Coast Highway in the Wrigley district, boasts artistic scenes, including hand-painted wooden cutouts of skaters on a plywood pond. The displays, primarily scaled-down Christmas cottages, have been erected between stately cedar trees wreathed in Christmas lights that stay on between 5 and 10 p.m. through Jan. 2.

11. TORRANCE
DORIS WAY, ROBERT AND REESE ROADS, CAROL AND LINDA
DRIVES AND SHARYNNE LANE

More than 200 homes in the Seaside Ranchos neighborhood sport unusually large displays of lights and decorations. This Sleepy Hollow area comes alive as neighbor vies with neighbor to display the most elaborate decorations. Flocks of children and carolers stop by the houses in the area bounded by Pacific Coast Highway, Calle Mayor, Anza Avenue and Sepulveda and Palos Verdes boulevards. PCH is closed from 6 to 10 p.m. nightly through Christmas to accommodate spectators. Enter Linda Drive by car from Palos Verdes Boulevard or enter Calle Mayor from Carlow and Vanderhill roads.

12. HAWTHORNE
4117 W. 138TH ST.

Gary and Dottie Williams are the talk of the town with the 11-foot Ferris wheel on their front lawn. A three-foot Santa turns the light-covered wheel, whose passengers are stuffed animals. Also positioned in the yard is a six-foot Santa and his workshop, a model train, lighted sleighs and reindeer, and 25,000 lights. A 22-foot Christmas tree stands atop a two-story garage.

13. INGLEWOOD
3RD, 4TH, 5TH AND HARDY STREETS

Twenty arches of metal and plastic piping, decorated with red and silver garlands entwined with lights, span South 5th Avenue between Century Boulevard and Arbor Vitae Street. Most residents have sprayed their yards with fake snow and put up decorations, including Nativity scenes and life-sized Santas and reindeer.

14. HANCOCK PARK
276 WINDSOR BLVD.

An invitingly chaotic display includes two full-sized sleighs filled with oversized gift boxes. Larger-than-life figurines of children, dogs, deer, rabbits and other creatures decorate the northeast corner of Windsor and 3rd Street, as do Christmas trees and a small creche.

301 RIMPAU BLVD.

About seven blocks farther west along 3rd Street, sightseers come upon two giant Nativity scenes, Christmas trees, deer, candy canes and figures of Santa, carolers and snowmen.

15. BEVERLY HILLS
9463 SUNSET BLVD.

As they have for more than a decade, the residents create a monument as they outline the contours of the mansion with single strands of lights. They plant poles in their yard and turn them into pyramids of lights to mimic a forest of glittering Christmas trees.

Japanese Gardens

Japanese gardens—among the area's most tranquil retreats—are popular venues for weddings and receptions.

----

1. UCLA HANNAH CENTER
10619 BELLAGIO ROAD, BEL-AIR

This two-acre hidden garden has flourished for more than 30 years within blocks of the Hotel Bel-Air and across the street from UCLA. It was created in 1959 by Japanese architect Nagao Sakurai for oilman Gordon Green Guilberson in memory of Guilberson's mother. Six years later, Broadway department store magnate and UC Regents Chairman Edward W. Carter and his wife, Hannah, who had bought the property, donated the garden to UCLA. A 400,000-year-old stone, called "jade rock," was brought here from Japan, along with 400 tons of rocks and boulders, the main gate, a teahouse, a shrine and bridges. Individual tours are given from 10 a.m. to 1 p.m. Tuesdays and from noon to 3 p.m. Wednesdays. Guided group tours can be arranged for Wednesday and Friday mornings. (310) 825-4574.

2. TILLMAN WATER RECLAMATION PLANT
SEPULVEDA DAM RECREATION AREA,
6100 WOODLEY AVE., VAN NUYS

In the midst of the San Fernando Valley, next to a modern sewage plant, lies an oasis—a lush 6 1/2-acre garden that demonstrates a positive use of reclaimed water. Amid the abundant greenery are waterfalls, lakes, streams, hand-carved stone lanterns and a teahouse. A dry Zen meditation garden—a small part of the main garden—features "tortoise island," a large grass mound rising out of a sea of pebbles and representing the animal, which symbolizes longevity. Tours by reservation only. (818) 756-8166.

3. YAMASHIRO RESTAURANT AND BERNHEIMER'S GARDEN
1999 N. SYCAMORE AVE., HOLLYWOOD

One of the best views in the city can be seen from this replica of a Japanese mountain palace. The sprawling restaurant, set in a Japanese garden with a 600-year-old pagoda, was built in 1913 as a private home for two brothers, Adolph and Eugene Bernheimer, importers of Asian art. The restaurant and gardens are often used as settings for films. Open daily. (213) 466-5125.

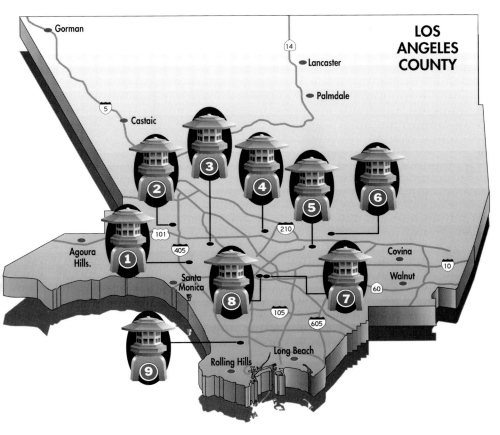

4. BRAND PARK
1601 W. MOUNTAIN ST., GLENDALE

In 1912, Leslie C. Brand, a Glendale founding father, was famous for the lavish celebrity fly-in parties he threw at his mansion. Private planes landed on Kenneth Road and taxied up El Miradero toward his estate. Today, the airstrip is a street, the mansion is an art and music library, and the estate is a park, complete with a Japanese teahouse and garden. (818) 548-3782.

5. HUNTINGTON LIBRARY AND GARDENS
1151 OXFORD ROAD, SAN MARINO

This five-acre garden has a 16th-century bonsai collection, carved votive stones representing Buddhist deities, an 18th-Century temple bell, drum and moon bridges, a dry Zen garden and a five-room Japanese house. The Japanese garden is one of the library's 12 gardens. Open noon to 4:30 p.m. Tuesday through Friday and 10:30 a.m. to 4:30 p.m. Saturday and Sunday. A donation of $4 to $7.50 is requested.

A couple strolls through the Japanese garden on the Huntington Library grounds.

Boris Yaro / Los Angeles Times

(818) 405-2275.

A few blocks away is the newly restored Japanese garden at the Ritz-Carlton Huntington Hotel, 1401 S. Oak Knoll Ave., Pasadena. The Picture Bridge, built in 1913, with its gabled roof, spans a stream feeding into the garden.

6. SIERRA MADRE ELEMENTARY SCHOOL
141 W. HIGHLAND AVE., SIERRA MADRE

A volunteer group of sixth-graders restored a 66-year-old Japanese garden and erected a marker about its history. In 1930, on the school grounds, Issei parents of about two dozen Japanese American schoolchildren built a traditional garden as a gesture of goodwill. During World War II, students vandalized the garden, which was never repaired. But after months of carwashes and bake sales, students completed the restoration project and unveiled the new garden in a formal tea ceremony. (818) 355-1428.

7. JAMES IRVINE GARDEN
JAPANESE AMERICAN CULTURAL AND COMMUNITY CENTER,
244 S. SAN PEDRO ST., LOS ANGELES

This 8,500-square-foot garden, also called Seiryu-En (Garden of the Clear Stream), is named for Irvine Ranch founder James Irvine, whose foundation contributed $250,000 of the initial $400,000 cost. Designed by landscape architect Takeo Uesugi, the garden sits at the edge of Little Tokyo with a stream that winds down a slope through flowers, bamboo and trees. Take the elevator down to the center's basement level and follow the corridor. Open from 9 a.m. to 5 p.m. weekdays and from 10 a.m. to 5 p.m. on weekends. (213) 628-2725.

8. NEW OTANI HOTEL
120 S. LOS ANGELES ST., LOS ANGELES

Overlooking downtown, this unusual half-acre garden is on the Garden Level (third floor) of the hotel. More than 50 types of plants, shrubs and trees grow around the walkways, ponds and waterfall. The Sado Island red stones come from the private collection of the late Yonetaro Otani, founder of the hotel chain. Open daily from 8 a.m. to 11 p.m. (213) 629-1200.

9. SHO FU EN (PINE WIND GARDEN)
TORRANCE CULTURAL ARTS CENTER,
TORRANCE BOULEVARD AND MADRONA AVENUE, TORRANCE

This beautiful 13,000-square-foot oasis of tranquillity with its streams, waterfalls and diverse and lush plantings, designed by Takeo Uesugi, was a gift from Epson America Inc. to the people of the South Bay area. (310) 781-7150.

Other notable Japanese gardens: Los Angeles County Museum of Art, Veterans Affairs complex in West Los Angeles, Cal State Long Beach, Cal State Dominguez Hills, Descanso Gardens in La Canada Flintridge and Rose Hills Memorial Park in Whittier. A Japanese garden show is held at the Nakaoka Memorial Community Center in Gardena every September.

Urban Oases

Paradise, if not lost, can be overlooked in L.A. But amid the clamor, tranquil gardens of earthly delights do exist.

----

1. ORCUTT RANCH
23600 ROSCOE BLVD., LOS ANGELES

Orcutt Ranch Horticultural Center is near the extreme northwestern "frontier" of Los Angeles in the Simi Hills, a half-mile down Dayton Creek Wash from the Ventura County line. Oil geologist William Orcutt built a Spanish-style ranch home there in the 1920s, and the house is now the centerpiece of 16 acres of rose gardens and citrus groves. Dozens of oak trees, many well over 500 years old, add their quiet dignity to the park. Open daily, 7 a.m. to 5 p.m. Free. (818) 346-7449.

2. DONALD C. TILLMAN GARDEN
6100 WOODLEY AVE., VAN NUYS

The Donald C. Tillman Japanese Garden is a 6.5-acre park that possesses an exotic charm. Open Monday through Thursday from noon to 4 p.m. A $2 donation per person is requested. Although it sits in the middle of the San Fernando Valley, the garden, which adjoins the Sepulveda Dam Recreation Area, is peaceful enough to be a nesting site for migratory birds. There is also a tiny lake. Black pines and peach and cherry trees set off three small "theme" gardens. (818) 756-8166.

3. VIRGINIA ROBINSON GARDENS
1008 ELDEN WAY, BEVERLY HILLS

County officials only give the location of this 6.2-acre gem when visitors call for a reservation. It is the smallest and the most recent addition (1982) to Los Angeles County's gardens. Virginia Robinson, the matriarch of the department store family, bequeathed the property to the county. She lived in the house on the property for 66 years until her death in 1977 at 99. Of special interest are the multi-terraced Italian Garden, adorned with statues and fountains, an herb garden and a palm garden covering two acres. (310) 276-5367.

4. DESCANSO GARDENS
1418 DESCANSO DR., LA CANADA FLINTRIDGE

Located at the foot of the oak and chaparral-covered San Rafael Hills, these idyllic gardens sprawling over 65 acres are visited by 150,000 people a year. A picnic area is just outside the gates, and the gardens include a 30-acre forest of oak trees

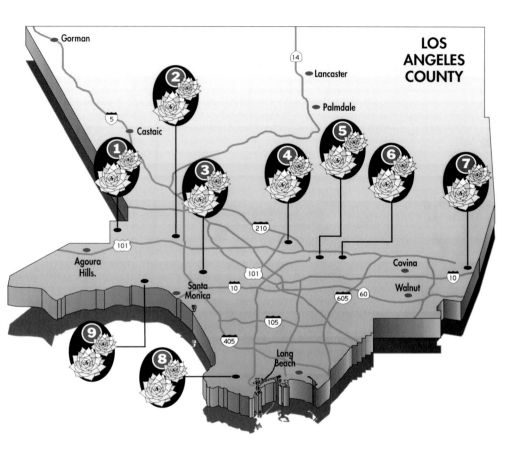

and camellia plants, a five-acre flower garden and a broad sample of plants native to California. A man-made lake lies at one edge of the gardens, and a stream winds down through a small canyon nearby. Walking paths are dotted with secluded spots. A tea room and gift shop are near the entrance. Open daily 9 a.m. to 4:30 p.m. Admission is $5 for adults. (818) 952-4400.

5. HUNTINGTON LIBRARY
1151 OXFORD ROAD., SAN MARINO

As the late Jack Smith, L.A. Times' columnist, wrote years ago, Henry Huntington "proved that the blood of Thoreau and Franklin ran in Huntington veins as well as that of Midas and Machiavelli." The vastly wealthy railroad and real estate magnate also proved to be sensitive, cultured and extremely generous. In 1919 he and his wife Arabella Duval Huntington deeded their San Marino estate and art collections to a nonprofit educational trust. The library and galleries contain objects from

Cassy Cohen / Los Angeles Times

Queen Anne Cottage is part of the 127-acre Los Angeles State and County Arboretum.

nearly every artistic medium plus rare historic artifacts. The grounds—207 acres, 130 devoted to botanical gardens—are well worth a separate visit. Open Tuesday-Friday, noon to 4:30 p.m., Saturday and Sunday, 10:30 a.m. to 4:30 p.m. Admission is $7.50 for adults, $6 seniors and $4 students. (818) 405-2100.

6. LOS ANGELES STATE AND COUNTY ARBORETUM
301 N. BALDWIN AVE., ARCADIA

This is the headquarters of the Los Angeles County Department of Arboreta and Botanic Gardens and, at 127 acres, the largest garden. Located on land that 100 years ago was E.J. (Lucky) Baldwin's ranch, this botanic garden has hosted up to 250,000 visitors annually. There are sections devoted to herbs, orchids, roses and plants native to Africa, Australia and California. Several historic structures are located within the Arboretum. The Queen Anne Cottage was made familiar to television viewers on the series "Fantasy Island." Open 9 a.m. to 4:30 p.m. daily. (818) 821-3222.

7. RANCHO SANTA ANA
1500 N. COLLEGE AVE., CLAREMONT

Probably the most rustic of the gardens, Rancho Santa Ana is just a mile or two from the steep south face of the San Gabriel Mountains. This garden was originally opened in Orange County in 1927, but it was relocated to Claremont in 1951. Rancho Santa Ana specializes in endangered plants and those native to semiarid Southern California. Strolling the winding paths, one can glimpse what this region's inland valleys looked like before they became heavily populated, permanently altering the ecosystem. Most of the space here is devoted to plants and trees, but there are

Rancho Santa Ana, probably the most rustic of the gardens, specializes in endangered plants and those native to semi-arid Southern California.

Lou Mack / Los Angeles Times

also a library of nearly 80,000 volumes and a molecular biology lab with a large collection of dried plant specimens. Open 8 a.m. to 5 p.m. daily. (909) 625-8767.

8. SOUTH COAST BOTANIC GARDEN
26300 CRENSHAW BLVD., PALOS VERDES PENINSULA

Most of the botanic garden's 87 acres were in use as a sanitary landfill until 1965, although planning and some planting began several years earlier. The soil thickness at the surface varies, but in places just a few feet of topsoil cover a layer of trash 100 feet deep. Scattered spots around the grounds are still settling—some up to 5 feet a year. Trellises sag, benches tilt, a small building containing restrooms is noticeably lower at one end. There is no danger but it does look odd. In addition to herb and vegetable gardens (produce is donated to the Meals On Wheels feeding program), there are bromeliads, roses, fruit trees and a desert garden with poppies, yucca and several species of cacti. And a large duck population gathers at the garden's small lake. This park is something of a secret by comparison to the other two large county arboreta which attract three to five times as many visitors annually. Open 9 a.m to 4:30 p.m. daily. (310) 544-6815.

9. SELF-REALIZATION FELLOWSHIP
17190 SUNSET BLVD., PACIFIC PALISADES

This surprising 10-acre enclave belonging to the Fellowship founded by Yogi Paramahansa Yogananda of India was opened in 1950. It exists happily as an exotic oasis in the midst of the Palisades. After visiting the shrine, visitors can stroll around a picturesque lake, view the Golden Lotus Archway and a replica of a 16th-century Dutch windmill. Or they can bask in a peaceful atmosphere dedicated to meditation, tolerance and cross-cultural appreciation. Open Tuesday through Saturday noon to 4:45 p.m. Admission free. (310) 454-4114.

You Pick 'Em Orchards

Bag 'em, box 'em or eat 'em on the spot: great pickings for weekend fruit harvesters all across the Southland.

---

1. PJK CHERRY FARM
45674 COPCO AVE., GORMAN

In a small valley among rolling hills—only 15 minutes from Magic Mountain—is a 20-acre peach and cherry orchard. Here, cherry season begins in early June with 700 trees bearing Bing and black tartarian cherries, which are sweeter and smaller than Bings. Peach season starts in late September according to ranch owner Paul Kish. Once you've picked your fill, at about $1 to $1.50 per pound, you can hike or fish at nearby Quail Lake. Orchard hours are from 7 a.m. to 6 p.m.

Take the Golden State Freeway north from Los Angeles and exit at Quail Lake Road. Turn right, go under the bridge, then turn right again at Copco Avenue. At the end of the road continue a little farther to the entrance and head toward the big barn. Call (818) 337-6498 or (805) 248-1177.
- **"From Ridge Route to Grapevine," see Page 181.**

2. MILLER'S CHERRY FARM
18540 PINE CANYON ROAD, LAKE HUGHES

Tom Miller, a retired makeup artist for the movie industry, and his wife, Sandy, a retired schoolteacher, tend to a variety of 250 cherry trees on their three-acre orchard. Tom prefers to sell his cherries to "people not in a hurry; and children and people in wheelchairs" are especially welcome because many of his trees' branches hang low. Customers are implored not to climb the trees or break the branches because the trees become susceptible to infection when scratched.

Take the Golden State Freeway north from Los Angeles to Lake Hughes Road and turn right. Drive 22 miles to where the road ends at Elizabeth Lake Road. Turn left: Miller's Ranch is around the corner, about a quarter of a mile. Opens around mid-June, from 8 a.m. to 5 p.m. Costs about $1 to $1.50 per pound. (805) 724-1728.

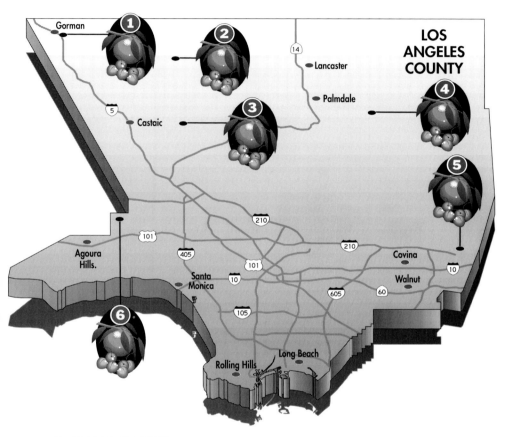

3. NESSA RANCH
38820 BOUQUET CANYON, LEONA VALLEY

A parade, usually in June, inaugurates the cherry season in Leona Valley, where 15 pick-your-own orchards can be found. Pick up a map at the general store or just follow the signs to find the orchards. Ranch owner Ken Striplin, like most other ranchers, provides ladders and buckets. Cherry season begins in May at the 60-acre Nessa Ranch. Juicy, ripe peaches and Asian pears are ready to harvest in mid-August. Prices average $1 or more per pound. Open weekdays from 9 a.m. to 2 p.m. and weekends from 8 a.m. to 5 p.m. Call (805) 270-1973.

The Leona Valley cherry-picking hot line is (805) 266-7116. Go north on I-5 from Los Angeles and take the Valencia Boulevard exit. Turn right (northeast) and go about four miles, then go left (north) to Bouquet Canyon, about 23 miles.

Cherry picking in
Leona Valley

4. ZINK'S RANCH
35609 80TH ST., LITTLEROCK

The aroma of the ripe apricot orchard on the Zink family's 12-acre ranch is delicious at the end of June. Apricots and peaches sell for 45 cents a pound. Asian and Bartlett pears begin to ripen the first week in August, and picking goes on for about a month. Bartletts sell for 25 cents a pound and Asian pears are about 65 cents a pound. Call (805) 944-1239.

Take California 138 (Pearblossom Highway) from the Antelope Valley Freeway and exit at 80th Street. Turn left (north) from Pearblossom Highway.

5. HERITAGE PARK
5001 VIA DE MANSION AVE., LA VERNE

Behind the park's 100-year-old Weber House are about 300 citrus trees. The self-serve harvest is meant to remind people of when the San Gabriel Valley boasted 40,000 acres of citrus groves and small farm crops, as well as to raise money for the park. Harvesters at the 1 1/2-acre park are assessed at about $4 for a 10-pound bag. Navel oranges can be picked between December and April. Valencia oranges are ready in April. Lemons are available year-round and a small pumpkin patch is full of tricks and treats in October. Call for an appointment, (909) 593-2862.

Take Foothill Boulevard east from Los Angeles, turn left (north) on Wheeler Avenue, then turn right (east) on Via de Mansion Avenue.

6. ORCUTT RANCH
23600 ROSCOE BLVD., WEST HILLS

This 25-acre orange and grapefruit orchard is run by the Los Angeles Department of Parks and Recreation. You can pick your own fruit from 8 a.m. to 5 p.m. the weekend after July 4. The fruit will be about $2 a grocery bag. Call (818) 883-6641 or (818) 883-8531.

Take the Hollywood Freeway north from Los Angeles to Valley Circle Boulevard (north) to Roscoe Boulevard and turn left (east).

From Ridge Route to Grapevine

Between Los Angeles and Bakersfield lies a stretch of Interstate 5 called the Grapevine. Most motorists believe the eight-lane freeway earned its name for the many curves it makes as it winds through the Tehachapi Mountains.

But few know of the real grapevines entwined in its history. Almost two centuries ago, Don Pedro Fages, a Spanish army lieutenant, noticed the abundance of Cimarron grapes growing wild in an area north of what is now Gorman and named the place Canada de las Uvas, or Grapevine Canyon. Don Pedro knew the area well, having long chased deserters through the rugged canyon at the southern end of the San Joaquin Valley. Wild grapes still grow in the area.

The Interstate 5 Grapevine is about 12 miles of road that has its origin in three earlier highways.

The first was a series of narrow footpaths used by Indians and later followed by the Spanish. The paths headed west from Newhall along the San Andreas Fault to Gorman, and north over the Tejon Summit.

In 1859 entrepreneurs widened the roadway to accommodate stagecoaches and freight wagons. Today, only a piece of this trail remains, beside the old Sierra Highway in Newhall.

Fifty years later, California engineers began planning a route that would shave 44 miles from the trip between Newhall and Gorman.

In 1915 the Ridge Route was opened, the first major highway connecting Los Angeles with the San Joaquin Valley. The road was a narrow ribbon of concrete with steep grades and 642 curves along the ridge top that stretched 39 miles through the Angeles National Forest.

It was hailed as a $3-million miracle of modern engineering, providing safety and a maximum speed of 15 m.p.h. But four years later, the road was considered "potentially one of the most dangerous in the world" because of the tight curves, steep grades and sharp drop-offs on both sides.

During the Roaring '20s, the small town of Grapevine in Kern County began to develop. The town was the final resting spot before and after travelers tackled the steep mountain road. Rockslides, tumbleweeds and potholes made trips a bit rough.

Drivers had to be ready to contend with flat tires and carsick passengers. Many automobiles would overheat, and wise travelers toted along some water.

On hot summer days, truck

The old "Grapevine" route really followed the ridges, as seen in this view looking south.

181

drivers would set the automatic throttle on their rigs and stand outside the truck on the running board to catch the breeze.

After dark, headlights along the Ridge Route formed a continuous chain as cars and trucks pulled into way stations, garages and cafes. Only the foundations remain from some of those stops—the Tumble Inn, Queen Nell's Castle, Martin's Place.

One of the most remembered landmarks was the Sandberg Lodge, a three-story log cabin built just before the Ridge Route was opened. The cabin was the centerpiece of a town near Quail Lake, built by and named after cattle rancher Harold Sandberg. The tiny town's amenities included a gas station and stables. The lodge had a dance floor, a few slot machines and a roulette wheel. The rancher was the town's postmaster, and he also ran "the crib," a brothel behind the cabin.

The town of Sandberg went into decline around 1933 when the Ridge Route was replaced by the three-lane Highway 99. But the community attracted attention in 1944 when newspaper accounts labeled Sandberg a "hotbed for seditionists." The FBI arrested a German mother and daughter for allegedly setting up a radio transmitter in the mountains and beaming military secrets to the Nazis during World War II.

All but one of Sandberg's buildings—the crib—burned in a 1962 fire. The crib was later hauled off to another ranch down the road to be used as a bunkhouse. But, according to ranch hands, it is haunted by a bluish ghost who appears to be female.

In the 1950s, Highway 99 was widened to a four-lane expressway, and 347 curves were straightened, eliminating eight miles of roadway.

Brake-check areas and ramps for stopping runaway vehicles were added. In the late 1960s, the road was rebuilt again, becoming Interstate 5.

In the spring, one of the state's most colorful displays of California poppies is visible from the Grapevine. In 1991 environmental artist Christo lined the route with 1,760 yellow umbrellas. But the exhibit was quickly dismantled after one of the huge umbrellas blew down and killed a sightseer.

As for the town of Grapevine, in the early 1960s about two dozen townsfolk moved to nearby Lebec. Today, it's just a truck stop with two gas stations, a restaurant and a few fast food places—only a mile from the remains of the town.

Playgrounds for City Slickers

From virtual reality to bungee jumping, L.A. County offers something for any urbanite in search of a thrill.

----

1. HOLLYWOOD ROCK WALK

GUITAR CENTER, 7425 SUNSET BLVD., HOLLYWOOD

They won't make you a star here, but you can look at their relics. The sidewalk of the Guitar Center's flagship store is to rock 'n' roll fans what the front walk at Mann's Chinese Theater is to movie fans. The handprints and signatures of such musical innovators as the Moody Blues, Stevie Wonder and Eddie Van Halen are embedded in individual paving blocks for a foothold in history.

Touring the Hollywood Rock Walk at the Guitar Center on Sunset Blvd.

Olivia Barrionuevo / Los Angeles Times

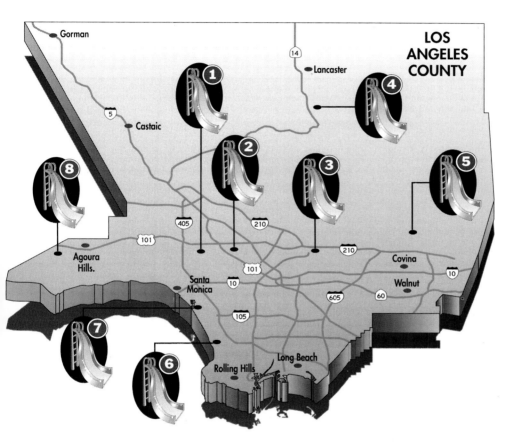

2. CITYWALK
1000 UNIVERSAL CENTER DR., UNIVERSAL CITY

The carnival-like atmosphere of shops, restaurants, street musicians, a giant video screen looming over an artificial beach and King Kong dangling over the entryway offers a playful ambience. Sandwiched between the Hollywood and Ventura freeways, it's open from 11 a.m. to 11 p.m. Most restaurants stay open later; parking is $6. (818) 622-4455.

3. VIRTUAL WORLD
35 HUGUS ALLEY, OLD TOWN PASADENA

This is the place for those waiting to dive through the canals of Mars or battle towering warriors from a cockpit of a three-story walking tank. On Friday and Saturday nights, reservations are often required for these big video games operated with complex controls. One 10-minute "inter-dimensional" ride costs $7 to $9, depending on the time and the day of the week. (818) 577-9896.

4. CALIFORNIA DRAG-RACING SCHOOL
LOS ANGELES COUNTY RACEWAY, 6850 E. AVE. T, PALMDALE

Ever feel like really putting the pedal to the metal? How about a $995 course in drag racing, where you can wheel around in a $20,000 dragster capable of doing a quarter-mile in eight seconds flat? Or you can take the family car out to the raceway any weekend and floor it all day long for $20. Since most insurance companies consider this a high-risk activity, they'll only insure your body, not your car. The dragstrip is in Palmdale, sandwiched between a cement company and the San Andreas Fault. (805) 533-2224.

5. BUNGEE JUMPING
NARROWS BRIDGE, AZUSA CANYON

Risking cuts, bruises and even death is all part of the thrill for some adrenalin fanatics. Licensed instructors with Bungee America take jumpers up a four-mile trail to the Bridge to Nowhere that arches about 250 feet above a spectacular gorge. The 60-year-old, 150-foot-long monument in San Gabriel Canyon, officially called the Narrows Bridge, was never completed. Plungers can enjoy the all-day outing for $40 to $115 a person, depending on the number of jumps. Reservations required; call (310) 322-8892. (For those who don't have all day, try the Queen Mary's 210-foot, 21-story bungee tower for $85 a jump. (310) 435-1880.)

6. HAMILTON GREGG BREWWORKS
58 11TH ST., HERMOSA BEACH

This do-it-yourself brewery offers amateurs over 21 access to the stainless steel kettles, hydraulic bottles and temperature-controlled fermentation room. Customers can choose among 45 beer styles, from light lagers to porters and stouts. Be ready to spend up to 2 1/2 hours mixing the brew in this bar-like atmosphere, then return in two weeks to fill and label the fruits of your efforts. Customers get 48 22-ounce bottles of beer for their trouble, at package prices ranging from $80 to $130, depending on the beer style. Open 5 to 11 p.m. Tuesday and Wednesday, 11 a.m. to 11 p.m. Thursday to Sunday. Validated parking. (310) 376-0406.

7. VENICE BOARDWALK
OCEANFRONT, VENICE

This 1.5-mile tourist-thronged boardwalk is where the stunt-skating dance team Bad Boyz helped make the walk the roller-blading, roller-skating capital of the world. Besides the renowned Muscle Beach where bodybuilders pump iron, Venice is known for its free-spirited and swimsuit-clad roller-bladers, poets, rap dancers, musicians and open-air shops.

8. ROCK STORE
30354 MULHOLLAND HIGHWAY, AGOURA HILLS

The fabled biker hangout in Agoura Hills picked up its "born to be wild" character in the 1960s when Steve McQueen cooled his leather riding boots there. Bikers can grab a beer or soft drink at this legendary store, built on a hill out of piled-up rocks. Members of the Hollywood biker crowd, including Sylvester Stallone, Jay

Leno, Mickey Rourke, Keanu Reeves, Peter Fonda, Eddie Murphy and Arnold Schwarzenegger, can sometimes be seen here.

Other popular hangouts: Third Street Promenade in Santa Monica, Melrose Avenue in Hollywood, the Planetarium laser show at Griffith Park Observatory, Greystone Park and Mansion picnic grounds in Beverly Hills.

IV.
CALAMITIES AND CATASTROPHES

We've saved the worst for last. Despite the chapter title, this is not an inclusive chronicle of local disasters. Just snapshots of ghastly happenings—fires, floods and quakes—and the scars they've left on the landscape and in collective memory. Shattering events that tore lives asunder while bringing others together in a community of crisis and necessary heroism.

But Southlanders are survivors, like the hardy dwellers on the Midwestern flood plains or in the hurricane alleys of the Southeast. Some brand us foolhardy souls, like those who rebuild their huts on the cooled lava of volcanic slopes. But we can count our blessings, along with all those afflictions that don't come calling—tornadoes and tsunamis, for instance, or plagues of locusts. And who's afraid of a Medfly?

Quake Faults

L.A.'s jagged coast, mountains and valleys were formed by quake faults; a tour of our bizarre topography.

1. TEJON PASS

This is one of three major Southern California mountain passes created by the San Andreas Fault, where the Golden State Freeway cuts through the heart of the fault zone. A band of black, pulverized rock is visible in the deep road cut. The fault can also be seen along Gorman Post Road, where a row of ponds marks the main trace of the fault.

2. ANTELOPE VALLEY FREEWAY

The road cut along the Antelope Valley Freeway exposes the spectacular action of the San Andreas Fault, where layers of sedimentary rock have been bent and contorted by compression—most recently by an 1857 earthquake whose magnitude is estimated at more than 8.0. To get the best view, park along Avenue S just west of the freeway and walk up the hill.

A cut in the Antelope Valley Freeway exposes the San Andreas Fault.

Rick Meyer / Los Angeles Times

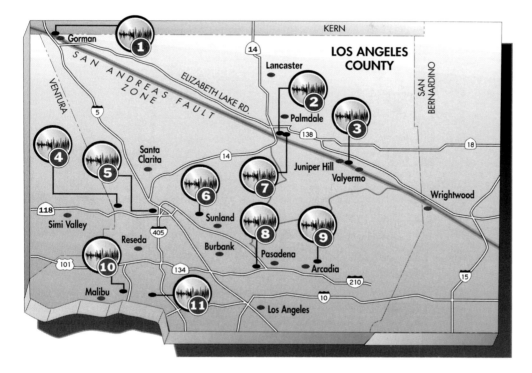

3. DEVIL'S PUNCHBOWL

Wedged between the San Andreas and Punchbowl faults, these 1,300 acres of tan and pink sandstone have been compressed, folded, broken, uplifted and eroded into a grand geological display dating back more than 12 million years. The rocks that were once horizontal have been tilted upright by compression between these two major faults. To see this wilderness area and nature preserve, take the Golden State Freeway to the Antelope Valley Freeway and exit at Pearblossom Highway, which joins California 138. Continue east to Pearblossom. Go south on Longview Road (County N6) and follow the county route and signs to Devil's Punchbowl County Park.

4. SIMI VALLEY FREEWAY SUMMIT

In the Chatsworth area, one of many small unnamed faults can be seen in the deep road cuts at the summit of the Simi Valley Freeway west of Topanga Canyon Boulevard. Look for offsets in the layered shale and sandstone. This area can be seen from the south side of the freeway, across from Call Box No. 4.

5. SYLMAR

To find the Mission Wells Fault in the San Fernando Fault zone, take the

Two contrasting rock types show clear line of fault in Pacoima Canyon.

Rinaldi Street exit of the San Diego Freeway. About three-quarters of a mile north of the exit, look for what is called a "zone of disruption," where gray shale rocks are dislodged from the hillside and, in some cases, crumble when picked up.

6. PACOIMA CANYON

A few yards off Little Tujunga Road is a microcosm of the natural forces that shaped the mountains. The San Gabriel Fault, exposed in the cliff face, lies between two massive rock formations. A few feet away, a small stream steadily erodes the cliff. To get there, take the Foothill Freeway to Little Tujunga Road and drive about 10 miles north. The area is identified by a Forest Service marker.

7. LAMONT ODETT OVERLOOK

Vivid evidence of the crushing and folding effects of fault action can be seen at this overlook, named for the former part-owner of the Antelope Valley Press Newspapers. It is at the edge of the San Andreas Fault zone overlooking Lake Palmdale off the Antelope Valley Freeway, about two miles north of the Pearblossom Highway exit. Northbound drivers can stop at the Vista Point turnout south of the Avenue S off-ramp. A plaque points out the fault line.

8. THE EAGLE ROCK

On the south side of the Eagle Rock Fault zone stands a 50-foot boulder whose configuration gave the community of Eagle Rock its name. Part of the 20,000-foot-deep fault runs along the back of the prominent rock. Take the Ventura Freeway to the Figueroa Street exit. Go south one block to Colorado Boulevard, turn east on

Colorado and then north on Patrician Way. Cross over the freeway, park before the street narrows and walk north about 100 feet. On the left side of the road, at the base of Eagle Rock, look for a change from pebbly sandstone to crushed rock.

9. ARCADIA WILDERNESS PRESERVE

In the foothills of the San Gabriel Mountains is a series of east-west trending faults known as the Sierra Madre Fault zone. A fault scarp can be seen on the west side of the preserve, about 200 feet upstream from the bridge. It appears as a sharp juxtaposition between two contrasting rock types. Take the Foothill Freeway to Santa Anita Avenue, drive north toward the mountains about one mile, turn right on Elkins Avenue and left on Highland Oaks Drive. The entrance to the park is about one mile north. The preserve is closed on weekends except by reservation.

10. TOPANGA CANYON

The Tuna Canyon Fault zone crosses Topanga Canyon. Drive 2.2 miles north of Pacific Coast Highway on Topanga Canyon Boulevard and park just north of the bridge at the entrance to the narrows of the Topanga Canyon. Look for an abrupt change from very light-colored sandstone to layers of a reddish-brown pebbly rock, or conglomerate, which look like they have been sliced.

11. BENEDICT CANYON

Along the San Diego Freeway, south of Getty Center Drive, look west for a change from light sandstone to a dark gray layered shale, showing where the Benedict Canyon Fault crosses the freeway about half a mile north of Sunset Boulevard.

■ **More Southland calamities, see below.**

SOURCE: Geologist and tour guide John Alderson of the Wilderness Institute.

One of California's Worst Disasters

The morning of March 12, 1928, the tender of the St. Francis Dam, Tony Harnischfeger, summoned engineer William Mulholland to tell him about muddy water escaping from the west embankment. After a two-hour survey, Mulholland declared that repairs were called for but that there was no immediate danger.

Harnischfeger, among others, had expressed concern about the safety of the dam, basically a giant concrete arch, on a number of occasions. He was so worried that he built stairs to a mountain behind his home as an escape route for his 6-year-old son and himself.

Harnischfeger and his son never had a chance to climb his stairs. They were among the first to die.

A few minutes before midnight, the 2-year-old St. Francis Dam crumpled, unleashing 11.7 billion gallons of water into the Santa Clarita Valley. It was one of California's worst disasters, with an official death toll—450—just two short of the 1906 San Francisco earthquake and fire.

A wall of water rushed down the narrow gorge of San Francisquito Canyon through Piru, Fillmore, Santa Paula and Ventura before reaching the sea 54 miles and 5 1/2 hours later.

Those who lost their lives included 42 students, half the enrollment at Saugus

The St. Francis Dam and the reservoir after its completion in 1926.

Los Angeles Times

The dam after it collapsed two years later.

Los Angeles Times

Elementary School. Some believed that the toll may have been even higher because many bodies, possibly scores of migrant Mexican farm workers, were washed into the ocean.

Nine hundred buildings were destroyed and 300 others severely damaged; 24,000 acres of agricultural and home sites were devastated. The cost in 1928 dollars was estimated at $20 million.

As chief engineer of the city's Bureau of Water Works and Supply, Mulholland considered himself responsible for the disaster. "Don't blame anybody else; you just fasten it on me," he said. "If there is an error of human judgment, I was the human."

Twelve days later, a hasty investigation found that his design was at fault. The once-celebrated engineer would spend his last years as a broken man.

Mulholland died on July 22, 1935, at age 79. More than a half-century later, in

1992, he was exonerated. After an exhaustive investigation, the Assn. of Engineering Geologists' Southern California Section issued a new study of the disaster. It concluded that the dam collapsed because its eastern edge sat on an ancient landslide that plowed into it "like a bulldozer blade," causing a chain reaction. Given geological knowledge at the time, the study said, Mulholland and his designers were not aware of the fatal flaw or able to recognize it in the investigation after the collapse.

Although the disaster cost Mulholland his reputation, his name remains a familiar one to Angelenos. There's Mulholland Drive and Mulholland Highway, San Fernando Valley's Mulholland Junior High School and a fountain at the intersection of Los Feliz Boulevard and Riverside Drive, where the engineer lived as a young man. And water still spills daily down the water system that first earned him his reputation and—for a few decades, at least—disgrace.

The Bel-Air/Brentwood Fire

It was an upwardly mobile disaster with its origins in a trash heap and its last gasp in some of the most exclusive real estate in Southern California.

Shortly after 8 a.m., a construction crew working in Sherman Oaks noticed the smoke and flames in a nearby pile of rubbish. Within minutes, Santa Ana winds gusting up to 60 m.p.h. would send burning brush aloft and ultimately sear Nov. 6, 1961, into Los Angeles' civic memory.

Life magazine called it "A Tragedy Trimmed in Mink," and glittering stars of stage and screen scrambled to do battle with the blaze that swept through Bel-Air and Brentwood that day.

Flaming embers danced from roof to wood-shingled roof, spreading the fire across the Santa Monica Mountains to the south and into the affluent Westside enclaves.

In Bel-Air, some film stars stood their ground against the encroaching flames. Maureen O'Hara risked her life to remain at her home and hose down her wooden roof. Fred MacMurray battled the flames and contained damage to just a portion of his home. But comedian Joe E. Brown saw his home burn to the ground. Burt Lancaster and Zsa Zsa Gabor also

In 1961, Linda Flora Drive in Bel-Air was in ruins after the fire.

Jim Hudelson / Los Angeles Times

lost their homes.

Former Vice President Richard M. Nixon and his chief researcher, Al Moscow, were working on a draft of Nixon's "Six Crises" when the flames threatened his rented house on North Bundy Drive. Nixon and Moscow took to the roof to water down the wood shingles, saving the home.

More than 300 police officers helped evacuate 3,500 residents during the 12-hour fire, and more than 2,500 firefighters battled the blaze, pumping water from neighborhood swimming pools to douse flames in some areas. Pockets of the fire smoldered for several days.

Even as firefighters battled what was to become the Bel-Air disaster, a separate fire had erupted simultaneously in Santa Ynez Canyon to the west, further straining local firefighting resources. That blaze was contained the next day after consuming nearly 10,000 acres and nine structures and burning to within a mile of the inferno raging in Bel-Air and Brentwood.

At least 200 firefighters were injured but no one was killed and more than three-quarters of the homes were saved.

Still, the fires were the fifth worst conflagration in the nation's history at the time, burning 16,090 acres, destroying 484 homes and 190 other structures and causing an estimated $30 million in damage.

Baldwin Hills: First Flood, Then Fire

It was Dec. 14, 1963, and people were still talking about President John F. Kennedy's assassination three weeks before. Residents were preparing for the holidays, and Revere G. Wells was on his rounds when he heard water gurgling through a leak somewhere in the Baldwin Hills Reservoir, which supplied water for 100,000 to 500,000 residents from mid-Los Angeles to the airport.

He discovered a crack in the 12-year-old dam about the width of a pencil.

Within three hours, as residents were frantically evacuated from the water's likely path, the crack had become a 75-foot-wide hole, gushing 292 million gallons of water that slammed into homes in its path. Most residents had been evacuated.

When the flood stopped 77 minutes later, five people had drowned, 8,000 people had been driven from their homes, 65 houses had been destroyed, more than 210 other apartments and houses had been seriously damaged to the tune of $12 million.

The hillside community had first become a household word in 1932, when it was the site of the Olympic Games' first-ever Olympic Village. But the dam tragedy, and another disaster in 1985, left the public with a different memory of the place.

On July 2, 1985, only blocks from the dam disaster, tragedy struck Baldwin Hills again. Flames roared up the hillside from road flares an arsonist had laid on a weed-filled hillside near La Brea Avenue just north of Stocker Street.

The blaze ripped through seven streets of the Baldwin Hills community, consuming 48 homes, damaging 18 others, causing $16 million in loss and leaving three people dead, including the mother of a firefighter who lived there.

The name of both the area and the dam that served it date to the 19th century, to a man named Elias Jackson (Lucky) Baldwin, a colorful entrepreneur who lived with an opulent disregard for Victorian conventions and was said to have survived two murder attempts by jilted lovers.

Before Baldwin bought the property, it had been part of the 4,000-acre Rancho

Water from
the ruptured
Baldwin Hills
Reservoir slams
through the
neighborhood on
Dec. 14, 1963.

UPI

La Cienega, owned by Vicente Sanchez, the alcalde, or mayor, of Los Angeles in 1830.
    When Sanchez died, the property was taken over by an heir, Tomas A. Sanchez,
the sheriff of Los Angeles County for nearly 10 years. Sanchez sold the ranch and it
eventually was purchased by Baldwin—who died in 1909, thinking that the ranch

The view from the Goodyear blimp west of La Cienega Boulevard as the Santa Monica Freeway was opened in 1965.

Larry Sharkey / Los Angeles Times

was a white elephant.

He couldn't have been more wrong.

In 1932, Olympic planners found the empty land an ideal site on which to build the Olympic Village, home base for 2,000 visiting athletes.

Five miles of streets were wrapped around the hills, and alongside them trim, pink-and-white prefabricated cottages were erected.

After the games, the cottages were knocked down. The Baldwin estate was eventually subdivided and developed with costly houses that by the late 1940s were making Baldwin Hills a well-to-do enclave.

Santa Monica Freeway: History and Hiatus

By the end of World War II, 280,000 people a year were flocking to what was rumored to be the land of milk and honey.

There was almost nowhere for them to live. Builders soon began answering the demand with thousands of homes, settling the city more densely and widely than it

Demolition crews working on the Santa Monica Freeway where a portion of it collapsed at Fairfax Avenue during the Northridge quake.

Iris Schneider / Los Angeles Times

had ever been.

Transportation had to match the population and real estate boom, and in 1947 the state Division of Highways began buying up property along the route that was to become the Santa Monica Freeway.

It would take nearly a decade and $98.5 million to purchase 4,129 parcels of land from churches, banks, markets, homeowners and even a railroad. Almost 15,000 people were displaced by the freeway.

One hundred property owners sued the state; only two ended up in court. Most residents along the freeway's path—and most civic leaders—were elated that the hoped-for Santa Monica Freeway was finally going to be built.

In 1957, with legal obstacles cleared, construction crews began to build Los Angeles' first east-west freeway, starting with the bridge that spans the Los Angeles River.

From the Santa Ana Freeway downtown to the ocean, the 17-mile freeway would eventually cost more than $210 million, or $12 million a mile, compared to $5 million a mile for the older Hollywood and Harbor freeways.

On Jan. 29, 1965, thousands of Angelenos—mostly Westsiders waiting for the linkup—stood watching as the 4.6-mile section of the Santa Monica Freeway from Vermont Avenue to La Cienega Boulevard was dedicated.

The dedication was zestful, even though the freeway was not finished. Instead of the usual ribbon-cutting, a tire dangling at the end of a 150-foot-long rope secured to the hovering Goodyear blimp tore through the ribbon just west of La Cienega Boulevard as a Dixieland band played.

A few days short of 29 years later, a section of the freeway just east of the ribbon-cutting site was destroyed by the Northridge earthquake. The freeway was back in action in less than three months.

Index

Acknowledgments

This book would not have been possible without the inspirational help of writers and editors like Bill Boyarsky, Sheila Daniel, Burt Folkart, Patt Morrison and Tim Rutten, and of my bosses, Carol Stogsdill, Leo Wolinksy and Lennie La Guire.

My deep appreciation goes as well to the many readers and colleagues who have contributed greatly to my stories: Erwin Baker, Ed Boyer, David Blume, Stan Chambers, Sue Ellen Cheng, Viola Cox, Siegfried Demke, Ashley Dunn, Margaret Farnum, Earl Gustkey, Scott Harris, Steve Harvey, Nieson Himmel, Karen Robinson Jacobs, Paul Lieberman, John Lucero, Eric Malnic, Bob Pool, Ray Ramirez, George Ramos, Joel Sappell, Rich Simon, Russ Snyder, Marty Tregnan and Larry Zuckerman.

Other friends and acquaintances in the history field have provided assistance in a variety of ways: David Cameron, Carolyn Kozo Cole, Glen Creason, Carolyn Garner, Roberta Greenwood, Barbara Hoff, Stone Ishimaru, Craig St. Clair, Dan Lewis, Stephen Sass and Thomas Sitton. A sizable thank-you is due to Marc Wanamaker for his photo archives and encyclopedic knowledge of Hollywood.

A special bow to Times librarian Steve Tice and former Times researcher Michael Meyers, who both deserve a share of credit for CURBSIDE L.A.

I thank the production team that worked with diligence and skill to create this book: Dan Pollock for editing; Tom Trapnell for design and cover work; Helene Webb, Rob Hernandez, Lorena Iiguez and Victor Kotowitz for mapmaking; Marilyn Shigetani, Ray Recendez, Jacquie Araujo, Rikki Sax and Dan Chodos for electronic photo expertise and retrieval; Cathy Irvine for promotional layout.

And I must not forget the Times photo librarians: David Cappoli, Chris Embree, Ed Natividad, Marcia Nunez-Valenzuela, Suzanne Oatey, Gay Raszkiewicz, Mildred Simpson, Laura Vinales-Simpkins and Laura Vgalde.

My apologies to any contributors whom I have omitted.

A final thank-you goes to my extremely patient husband, Jim, and children, Christina, Michael and Jamie.